DEFENSIVE REVOLVER FUNDAMENTALS

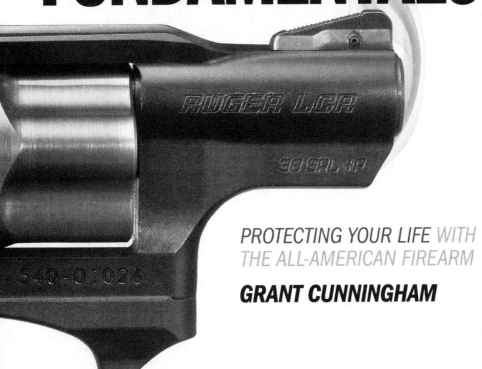

PROTECTING YOUR LIFE WITH
THE ALL-AMERICAN FIREARM

GRANT CUNNINGHAM

Published by

Gun Digest® Books, an imprint of F+W Media, Inc.
Krause Publications • 700 East State Street • Iola, WI 54990-0001
715-445-2214 • 888-457-2873
www.krausebooks.com

To order books or other products call toll-free 1-800-258-0929
or visit us online at www.gundigeststore.com

ISBN-13: 978-1-4402-3695-2
ISBN-10: 1-4402-3695-X

Cover Design by Al West
Designed by Sharon Bartsch
Edited by Corrina Peterson

Printed in the United States of America

Contents

SECTION ONE: OPERATING THE REVOLVER

SECTION TWO: USING THE REVOLVER IN SELF DEFENSE

Foreword

by Rob Pincus

When Grant Cunningham and I first met (over the internet, of course), I was immediately confused. His thoughts in regard to training were modern, insightful and refreshing. But, his website was full of revolver pictures. Those two things don't normally go together. The first center-fire handgun that I spent any significant amount of time with, and the gun that I really learned to shoot with, was a Smith & Wesson Model 19 "Combat Magnum." As the son of a 1970's cop, revolvers were the only serious defensive handgun option. Naturally, I shot .38s out of it most of the time. The Model 19 still holds a special place in my heart and, to this day, I carry S&W revolvers (albeit J-Frames) for defensive purposes from time to time. Over the past few years there has been a resurgence of interest in the viability of the revolver as a legitimate choice for personal defense. This resurgence happened to coincide with a few key things in my world.

First, I had gotten rather complacent in regard to "probable threat profiles" and the likelihood of actually needing more than five shots out of a snubnosed revolver during the several years I lived in the imaginary village of Telluride, Colorado, and had been carrying a S&W 642 more often than any other gun.

Second, I was trying to more publicly skew my defensive firearms teaching and advice towards what actual was happening in the real world, as opposed to playing towards the (seldom seen in the actual firearms owning public) "one gun is no guns, carry three spare mags and two flashlights" type of Tactical Readiness Rhetoric that had taken over some aspects of our community's discussions over the preceding decade. In the real world, lots of people carry small revolvers.

Third, I had met, and started spending time with, Grant Cunningham.

It turned out that the reason Grant had all those wheel-gun pictures on his web-site was because he is pretty much the Greatest Living Revolversmith. Before that goes to Grant's head too much, let's put that grandiose statement in perspective: In the 80s you could've easily started fist fights over trying to award that title to any-one… but, in the second decade of this century, there simply aren't many people even vying for the title. The fact is that much of our community has dismissed the revolver as a viable option. The cutting edge of firearms development, defensive training and even our media coverage has left the wheelgun behind. Does this mean that the title of "Greatest Living Revolversmith" is easy to earn? Absolutely not, quite the contrary: To even make a living as a revolversmith nowadays means you must be something special! Grant's work as a technician and as an artist is a product of his knowledge, meticulousness, passion and dedication to what some probably think of as a lost art. His work is so good, in fact, that he is bringing back the defensive revolver as an option for some of us that grew up with them and even introducing the younger generation to the fact that the option exists. I still carry that same 642 from time to time… but, now that it has been worked on by Grant, I promise you that I enjoy shooting it much more often than I did a decade ago! Grant's ability as a craftsman isn't what this book is about, however, so it shouldn't be what this foreword is about either. This book is about choosing, training with and using the revolver as defensive tool. I think it is important to note that Grant's knowledge, meticulousness, passion and dedication to the revolver as a craftsman heavily inform his opinions as an instructor in the art and science of using a revolver as a defensive tool. It is important to understand the incredible amount of detail, depth of research and thought that has gone into this book. Grant is an established expert and has been for many, many years. Yet, if you look at what he teaches, you see new information, progressive concepts and cutting-edge insight. Grant has continued to evolve and spends at least as much time working through pages of research and experimenting with training doctrine as he does filing metal and polishing parts. In 2009, when it was time for me to add a Defensive Revolver DVD to the Personal Defense Network library, I tapped Grant. The revolver might be your grandfather's tool, but PDN isn't your grandfather's training resource. I needed to find a balance between the old and the new. I needed someone who truly understood the revolver as a mechanical device and could apply post-modern training concepts to it's use. Grant Cunningham was the only real option and I am indebted to him for working with me to produce that DVD.

It would be disingenuous to omit the fact that Grant is a certified Combat Focus® Shooting Instructor from this essay, especially as he is one of the leader's in our CFS Community. In fact, it would not be an understatement to say that he has been one of the most influential instructors in the program. His ability to communicate information, especially the way he can distill the essence of a concept from a cumbersome explanation and efficiently get a student to grasp the important principles, is certainly the trait that has made him an invaluable asset to our cadre of teachers. That ability to communicate spans his spoken presentation and his written words, the latter of which you are about to experience. Over the years that Grant and I have known each other, he has certainly taught me much about the revolver, about teaching and about our community. It is a great honor to introduce him to those of you who aren't already familiar with his work, and to share my thoughts with those of you who already know how valuable he is to anyone who would consider the revolver as a defensive tool. Enjoy this book the first time through, then go back and revisit the details. The defensive revolver isn't an antiquated afterthought. It is a legitimate option that deserves a progressive and practical training approach, which is exactly what Grant presents in this book.

Train well!

Rob Pincus
Owner, I.C.E. Training Company

Acknowledgments

I'm lucky to have a wide circle of talented people on whom I can call when working on a project such as this. I appreciate each and every one of them.

First, many thanks to Rob Pincus for writing the Foreword and allowing me to reprint his superb essay "Respectful Irreverence" in the Appendix. Rob is a dedicated proponent of evidence-based training, and much of his work has been devoted to bringing real science to the study of armed response. He has inspired by example as to how we can and should question common knowledge and evolve our thinking on the subject of self defense. I have been one of those so inspired, and it's accurate to say that this book would not have happened had we not met a few years back.

Massad Ayoob, as always, gave me the benefit of his experience in the chapter dealing with the legal aspects of use of force. If there is anyone who knows more about that subject than Mas, I have yet to meet him. I'm grateful that he gave of his valuable time to review that section and supply much-needed feedback.

The photographs would not have been possible if not for the selfless time given by the models who played various roles, including Carl Fitts, Grant Fitts, Maurice Rahbani, Georges Rahbani, Liliane Rahbani and Hoda Rahbani. With the exception of my wife, master gunsmith Todd Koonce has the singular distinction of appearing in every book I've so far written; this time he plays one of the many bad guys pictured. It would seem I can't write a book without Todd.

Speaking of my wife, you'd think she'd get tired with all of the stuff I do - but such is not the case. She's a steadying influence on me and keeps me well fed and clothed while I toil away over a hot keyboard. I can't thank her enough for the wonderful years we've had together and just hope that she continues to put up with me!

Trent Cooper with Crossbreed Holsters was kind enough to provide one of their new J-frame appendix carry holsters for me to use for the pictures in the chapter on drawing the revolver. Crossbreed is a great company, making superb products with unmatched customer responsiveness. Thanks, Trent.

Thanks also to Don Fredrickson at Skyline Ford in Salem, Oregon, who provided some of the vehicles used in the pictures.

Finally I must thank my editor, Corrina Peterson, and the rest of the great team at F+W Media/Gun Digest Books. Behind every successful writer is a good editor, and Corrina's one of the best. She and her crew manage to glue together my scribblings and snapshots to produce good books, with nary a complaint. I wish I had their patience and talent!

THE WORST-CASE SCENARIO
WHAT WE TRAIN FOR AND WHY

An escalating incident takes time, has an aspect of mutual agreement.

Those who have chosen to arm themselves, whether in their home or legally on the street, face the prospect that someday, somewhere, they may have to shoot someone in justifiable self defense.

That's what this book is about.

Defensive fights, as violence expert Rory Miller points out[1], are idiosyncratic things; no two are alike. A lethal force incident is no doubt the pinnacle of all defensive encounters, but reason suggests that even at the top there is a hierarchy of severity, a scale of danger and our response to it.

It's possible to get into a shooting situation knowing ahead of time that you may have to shoot. The loudmouth who accosts you in the parking lot over a disputed space may escalate his actions from simple shouting to an assault with a deadly weapon. You may start with a conciliatory, concessionary posture, all the while planning your response should things get worse. You have some indication ahead of time that you might need to employ your firearm, giving you time to work out the details in your mind. We're not talking about a whole lot of time, mind you, but enough to prepare for what might come, to be proactive in terms of your readiness to engage your attacker.

From a training point of view, this kind of incident - the anticipated fight, or 'social violence' - is relatively straightforward to deal with, and thus is the kind of incident many defensive shooting courses prepare their students to face. It lends itself to assembly-line training and choreographed drills.

The problem is that it also appears to be the least common kind of deadly force encounter that we're likely to face. Rory Miller contends that attacks happen "closer, faster, more suddenly and with more power than most people can understand."[2]

The best database of private sector self-defense shootings that I know of has been compiled by Tom Givens, the founder and co-proprietor of Rangemaster in Memphis, TN. Tom has had more verified students involved in defensive shootings than anyone else, and he's taken pains to document every one of them - over 60, as this is being written. He's also appeared in a Personal Defense Network training video called "Lessons From The Street," where he recounts several representative cases from his files.

This work is unusual because the victims he interviews are people that have trained with him previously. Tom is a superb instructor, and it's safe to assume that his students are more aware and prepared for violence than the average person on the street. Yet they still became victims; the difference between them and the untrained victims common to the rest of Memphis is that Tom's students were able to fight back and win in all but two cases - and in those two cases the victims were not armed at the moment they were attacked.

The defenders were living their lives and minding their own business one moment, and in the next were faced with a life-or-death decision.

Living your life leaves you open to many ordinary, everyday distractions which can be exploited by an attacker.

What might come as an eye-opener to many people is that his students were almost always surprised by their attackers. There wasn't an overly extended eye contact period where the attacker and his prey were sizing each other up, or a protracted testosterone-fueled dance of one-upmanship. The defenders were living their lives and minding their own business one moment, and in the next were faced with a life-or-death decision. This is how attacks happen, both for Tom's students and for us.

Note that I didn't use the word *fight*. That word implies a certain level of voluntary participation by both parties. I use the word attack specifically because that's what happens: one person attacks another, who is forced to either defend or capitulate.

This book is about choosing to defend yourself from the surprise criminal attack. It's about that very short period of time - measured in seconds - when you find your life in imminent danger and lethal force is the correct response. It's also the most difficult kind of incident to prepare for and is too rarely discussed in CCW or defensive shooting courses.

Imagine: you're deciding between onion rings and french fries one moment, and the next suddenly needing to shoot someone. The surprise attack, the ambush, is the worst-case scenario we'll be considering throughout this book.

The skills necessary to go from zero expectation of lethal force to actually shooting a second or two later are very different from those needed when you can see it coming and have the opportunity to get ready.

We focus on this because the skills necessary to go from zero expectation of lethal force to actually shooting a second or two later are very different from those needed when you can see it coming and have the opportunity to get ready. This is reactive shooting in its truest sense, and is routinely ignored in much of the defensive shooting instruction currently available.

WITHOUT WARNING: SKILLS ON DEMAND

If you knew that you were going to need to shoot someone in the next fifteen seconds or so, your brain would have time to decide what it was going to do, what neurons it would fire and in what order, to accomplish the task[3]. Your brain prepares itself.

On the other hand, if you're attacked without warning or expectation your brain doesn't have that time to get ready, to pre-tense muscles and get into its fighting stance. Your body's natural and instinctive reactions, happening as they do without cognitive thought[4], will be your first indication that something is wrong. The effectiveness of your response has a lot to do with how efficiently you convert those

The target shooter's stance, with artificial alignment and positioning, doesn't often happen - if it ever does - in reactive defensive shooting.

instinctive reactions into intuitive responses, and is something that you don't do when you have any amount of early warning.

What good are those finely honed skills when you can't employ them because the situation has exceeded their utility?

Response to a predatory ambush looks nothing like the target shooting or competition stance, because our bodies have evolved reactions to efficiently deal with lethal threats.

Skills that are applicable for those instances when you have preparation time - getting into just the right stance, holding the gun just so, and finding the perfect sight picture - usually go right out the window when the threat has suddenly appeared in your face. Now you don't have the right stance or the right grip and perhaps can't even see your sights clearly. What good are those finely honed skills when you can't employ them because the situation has exceeded their utility?

On the other hand, if you practice skills that are applicable to the ambush attack, skills that work when you don't have time to get yourself ready, you'll

Data show most defensive shootings occur between three and five yards, or beyond two arms' reach.

Most defensive shootings happen outside of two arms' reach; inside that range a different range of skills is needed.

be prepared to deal with this worst-case scenario. What's more, you can still function at other levels of expectation, in that kind of incident where you do have a little time to see the attack coming and think about it.

THE WORST-CASE SCENARIO

That's why this book will deal with the worst-case scenario: the sudden, chaotic and threatening criminal attack. We'll look at how the body reacts in those cases, how to work with the body's natural reactions, and how to train realistically to convert those instinctive reactions into intuitive responses.

We'll be limiting the scope to attacks that occur beyond about two arms' reach. First, because most attacks happen outside of that limit[5], and second because the skills needed inside that range are more dependent on things other than shooting. Those inside-of-two-arms'-reach skills are still important, and I recommend that you take a class in dealing with them, but in most of the cases in which you're likely to need to employ your revolver you'll be further away.

The first section of this book deals with the hardware itself: how to shoot it, carry it, reload it and manipulate it. Readers of my first book, *Gun Digest Book of the Revolver*, will notice many similarities. The book you're now reading, though, is more focused on revolver handling from the defensive point of view. I'm interested in the most efficient, error-resistant methods I can find to protect my life and the lives of my students, and that's what you'll find here. Every aspect of how to handle the revolver has been evaluated not for how well it works in a shooting contest, but how well it's likely to work when your hands are shaking and sweating because someone is trying to do you harm. (If you need more in-depth information on the revolver itself, may I be so bold as to suggest you get a copy of *Gun Digest Book of the Revolver* if you haven't yet done so?)

The first section, then, is concerned with how to operate the revolver.

The second section deals with how to use the revolver to protect your life or the life of your loved ones. Personally, I've gone through quite a metamorphosis over the last decade or so regarding self defense training, and what you'll read is what I feel is the best information I have at this point in time. The section is based, in large part, on the Combat Focus® Shooting (CFS) program from I.C.E. Training, for which I'm a certified instructor.

Why Combat Focus® Shooting? First, because it's built on science and observable fact. It starts with the realities of how attacks happen; not the way we wish they'd happen or the way television tells us they happen, but how objective evidence tells us they do. CFS then takes into account the science of threat response, the medical evidence and research into how we survive violent attacks.

The responses that we choose - the tactics, in modern parlance - must work both with reality and with what our bodies can do. That's the basis of Combat Focus® Shooting.

Second - and as strange as this may sound - that hard-nosed focus on reality leads the course to respect the revolver. We know that revolvers save lives every day, and have for about a hundred and fifty years, so a course that doesn't work for a revolver is by definition not based on reality.

In most shooting schools the revolver is relegated to beginning-level

The author teaching a Combat Focus® Shooting class.

students. Many schools supply guns to their newest pupils, and the revolver is often what they issue. As the students advance they're allowed (and usually encouraged) to 'move up to' an autoloading pistol, thus establishing the notion that only beginners use revolvers. After all, the instructor is wearing a custom autoloading pistol - not a lowly revolver.

It's not unusual to find the more advanced courses reinforcing that attitude and passively discouraging their students from bringing their revolvers by intimating that, with a revolver, they will have trouble keeping up with the rest of the students. Some are blatant about it; there are actually instructors and schools out there that forbid revolvers in anything but beginning classes.

Those who aren't quite so bigoted often accommodate the wheelgun by making their courses 'revolver neutral': artificially limiting their strings of fire or requiring that shooters of high capacity autoloaders fill their magazines only partway. The revolver shooter rightly feels that they're holding the rest of the class back, which can feel like an embarrassing position to be in. It's also unrealistic training for the autoloader owners, so everyone loses.

The more astute reader will see the intellectual discord: we have a century and a half of history that clearly shows the revolver to be a satisfactory defensive tool in most regards, yet the average defensive shooting school would have us believe that they're useful only for the least skilled. Something's wrong with that point of view.

The objective historical evidence says the revolver is a proven defensive tool. To artificially penalize its use in a class devoted to using defensive tools

In most shooting schools, "advanced" students are encouraged to use autoloading pistols.

seems untenable to me. If the revolver works in the real world - and it's obvious that it does - then it should also work in training. If it doesn't, *then the training doesn't reflect reality!*

Combat Focus® Shooting acknowledges the fact that the revolver is still an efficient and effective choice and puts it through the same evidence-based curriculum as the autoloader. Yes, the revolver has its limitations; I've never shied away from acknowledging that the revolver shooter needs to be aware of those limitations, accept them and train accordingly. All handguns are compromises in some way, and the revolver is hardly an exception. But that doesn't mean it isn't effective or is unsuited for self defense. We know better.

This focus on realistic training, training that reflects the circumstances under which the handgun is most likely to be used, is why the revolver still has value and is why CFS doesn't need to penalize or 'level the playing field' to fit a revolver into class. Rob Pincus, the founder of I.C.E. Training and the author of the foreword to this book, understands this very well; his personal primary defensive handgun is often a five-shot snubnose revolver. I think that speaks volumes about the curriculum he's put together in Combat Focus® Shooting.

I submit to you that training that doesn't reflect reality is less likely to be of value when you have to shoot in self defense. Combat Focus® Shooting is congruent with history, observed reality and medical science. That's why I teach the course, and why I use it as the basis for what you'll read in these pages.

This is not, however, a Combat Focus® Shooting manual. There are many concepts in a CFS class that we won't touch on in this book, and there are some things I've added here that are congruent with CFS methodology and philosophy but aren't part of the official curriculum. I encourage you to take a Combat Focus® Shooting class (whether from me or one of the other Certified Instructors) in order to get the full experience.

Chapter 1

A WORD ABOUT
SAFETY

Firearms are dangerous things - that's why we use them to protect ourselves and our loved ones! It is precisely because of the danger they pose that they make good tools to stop bad people from doing bad things to good people. That is, if they're used properly.

Used improperly they present a danger to the user or to innocent people. That's not what we as conscientious, competent, law-abiding gun owners wish to have happen and why we approach all handling of firearms with safety first and foremost in our minds.

Guns always pose the same amount of danger, but the risk (the chance of that danger affecting us) changes. We create that change in risk through the use of safety rules and procedures. Following those rules and procedures ensures that the benefit of handling or using the gun outweighs the risk.

For instance, shooting a revolver makes an extremely loud sound and poses a very real danger to your hearing. You reduce the chances of that happening - your risk - by wearing good hearing protection. By doing so you reduce the risk to well below the benefit you'll get from shooting that gun, whether that benefit is simply recreational or in preparation for saving your life.

For any drill that you do, or wany class that you take, the benefit of doing or taking has to outweigh the risk involved.

Whether I'm teaching a class or simply handling a gun, I reduce the risk to myself and the people around me by following, and making sure everyone else follows, these easy-to-remember rules:

We reduce the risk of ear damage by wearing hearing protection so that we may benefit from training or practice.

1) Always keep the muzzle pointed in a generally safe direction.

A generally safe direction is one where, should the gun inadvertently discharge, it will not hurt you or anyone else. This changes from environment to environment, and requires that you always think about the safe direction.

2) Always keep your trigger finger outside of the triggerguard until you are actually in the act of firing.

The preferred place is straight along the frame above the trigger.

3) Always keep in mind that you are in control of a device that, if used negligently or maliciously, can injure or kill you or someone else.

This means that you must always think about what your target is, where your bullets will land, and all the other things that could result in your gun causing human suffering.

Safety is your most important responsibility. Whenever you pick up a gun, think about what you're doing and why. Reduce your risk, and help those around you reduce theirs by teaching them these rules.

Chapter 2

THE REVOLVERS ADVANTAGE IN DEFENSIVE SHOOTING

Even in this age of the polymer wonder pistol, the revolver has some advantages that are not easily dismissed.

C ritics of the double action revolver love to point out that it is old. Yes, it is! It is the oldest handgun design still being widely used, for everything from plinking to hunting to this book's subject of self defense.

That age, however, doesn't affect the fact that it is still a viable choice even in this twenty-first century age of the polymer autoloader. The revolver possesses some traits that are unique and present very real advantages when used as a protection tool.

SOME OF THE REVOLVER'S MANY ADVANTAGES

The revolver's first advantage is efficiency; the revolver requires no manipulation of the gun beyond operating the trigger in order to fire. There are no extra buttons or levers to push, which means that there are no buttons or levers to forget to push.

I've watched even highly-trained and experienced shooters forget to deactivate the safety on their autopistols when faced with a new and distracting shooting challenge. I've also seen them forget to activate that safety and negligently discharge their guns. These aren't people who are new to the guns, either. I'm talking about people with hundreds of hours of formal training, some of them police officers who are tasked with training their fellow officers. The more complicated something is, the easier it is to forget something when you're distracted.

The revolver is efficient, as there is only one control to manipulate to fire a shot: the trigger.

Part of the revolver's legendary reliability is the fact that it will function with any ammunition in its caliber; autoloaders, in contrast, are often very picky about bullet weight, shape and velocity.

That simplicity has a real advantage when the gun is used for home defense, where it might be used by family members who aren't intimately familiar with shooting. Naturally I recommend that everyone in your household be thoroughly trained, but even with training the very simple manual of arms of the revolver still makes it easier to use for someone who isn't going to practice every weekend. The revolver remains the easiest handgun to shoot, but that also has a downside (more on that later.)

Another major attribute of the revolver is reliability; the revolver will generally have a longer mean time between failures than that of even the best autoloaders, meaning that it will shoot more rounds without having mechanical issues that affect its operation. Of course that's not to say that revolvers never malfunction, only that they do so less often than a self-loading handgun. What's more, most of the malfunctions that can occur are easily prevented through proper technique or maintenance.

Part of that reliability is the fact that the revolver will shoot a much wider variety of ammunition. With an autoloader it's necessary to thoroughly test the gun with any specific type of ammunition because they are somewhat picky about bullet weight, shape, and velocity. Many experts hold that an autoloader should be tested with 200 rounds of any ammunition that you expect to use (which today would run into an awful lot of money).

In contrast, the revolver doesn't care about those things. If the cartridge is of the proper caliber the revolver will be able to shoot it, a fact which greatly eases the reliability testing requirements. I usually recommend firing several cylinders of the ammo in question just to make sure that a) ignition is consistent and b) that its point of impact agrees with the sights on the gun. That's a small amount and is significantly easier to afford.

A malfunction that requires clearing is quite rare with a revolver. While there is a malfunction drill (and I'll show it to you in a later chapter), I've personally never had to use it in the many tens of thousands of rounds I've fired through my revolvers.

From an operational standpoint, a revolver doesn't suffer from induced failures. By that I mean malfunctions that are caused (or significantly aided) by the shooter. The most common induced error in an autoloader is the jam caused by 'limp wristing.' The auto requires a certain amount of resistance to its recoil in order for the slide to reciprocate, eject and load another round. If the shooter can't maintain a perfectly solid grip, as when injured or extremely fatigued, the autoloader is likely to stop functioning. This isn't an issue with the revolver

The revolver is resistant to induced malfunctions, as when shooting around loose clothing.

The revolver can be disabled by a determined attacker who can hold the cylinder from turning; this is a weakness the revolver shares with the autoloader.

because the motive force comes solely from the trigger finger of the shooter.

While this book isn't concerned with shooting inside of two arms' reach, the revolver has a definite advantage when in contact with an attacker: it doesn't have a slide that can be inadvertently pushed out of battery, keeping it from firing. A slide can also be slowed by the clothing of you or your adversary, causing a jam. This particular advantage also works when shooting from inside of a coat pocket or an off-body-carry arrangement such as a holster purse. Those situations are extremely rare, but they serve to illustrate the versatility and resiliency of the revolver as a defensive tool. The revolver will simply keep shooting under those kinds of extreme conditions.

It's important to note that both the revolver and the autoloader can be rendered inoperable by a knowledgeable criminal who manages to get his hands on the gun, but at that point you have a new and more important problem: keeping the gun in your possession!

Part of being an efficient shooter in the context of self defense is being able to control the gun, and nothing makes that easier than a good match between the grip and your hand. The revolver, more so than the vast majority of autoloaders, makes it easy to get a good fit simply by changing the grips. Because the revolvers' grip size and shape isn't dictated by the need to fit a magazine, there is much more leeway in how big or how small the grip can be made. In many cases it's possible to take a revolver which doesn't fit the shooter well, make a grip change and end up with a combination that works well.

This is true regardless of whether the gun is too small or too big for the hands. Larger and smaller grips are available, and in extreme cases it's possible for a gunsmith to modify the grip frame to make an even greater change.

Of course, there are no magazines necessary to operate the revolver, which is an often-unappreciated advantage. Magazines are the weak spot for the autoloading pistol - they're fragile, they wear out, they're expensive and you have to remember to bring the darned things! A recent article from Jon Farnham[6], a noted defensive shooting instructor, talked about the advantage of not needing a magazine when grabbing a gun and running out of the house. While that's

The revolver doesn't need anything other than ammunition to function.

The revolver, simply by changing grips, can be made to fit a wide variety of hands and preferences.

not a terribly plausible event, it underscores the advantage of needing only ammunition to operate.

A very real advantage in an adrenalin-charged incident is the long and heavy trigger offered by the revolver. Understand that I teach my students to keep their fingers off the trigger until they're ready to shoot, and to get that finger off the trigger when they stop shooting, but we all know that the real world sometimes isn't like the classroom. In the confusion of a defensive shooting, there is the very real possibility that fingers will stray into the triggerguard, and there are enough videos of trained police officers inadvertently discharging rounds when in a tense situation - sometimes resulting in death. I would never suggest relying on a heavy trigger as a safety device, but must also acknowledge that it does provide another layer of protection to even the best safety habits.

WHEN THE REVOLVER ISN'T AN IDEAL CHOICE

This is a book about the revolver and its use in self defense, but I would be remiss if I didn't touch on some of the reasons you might not want to carry or use one.

I stated earlier that the revolver is the easiest handgun to shoot, and that's true; simply stroke the trigger and the gun will fire. While it's the easiest to shoot, it's the most difficult to shoot well. That heavy trigger, and the amount

Some people with lessened hand strength may have trouble with the heavy trigger of the revolver, sometimes to the point that they must use two fingers on the trigger.

The revolver isn't always the only choice, even for someone with strength issues. Racking an autoloader slide is easy once proper technique is learned and shouldn't be considered an obstacle.

of travel it has, requires dedication to really master. You can hand the revolver to anyone and they can shoot it, but that doesn't mean they'll be able to deliver the necessary accuracy to stop a threat efficiently.

That heavy trigger is also difficult for many people to even manipulate. People with very thin, non-muscular hands may be unable to fire the double action revolver. Revolvers often end up in the hands of students who've concluded (whether it's valid or not) that they don't have the strength to operate the slide of an autoloader. In my experience, that's exactly the opposite of the decision that should be made.

I can show a very frail person how to use body mechanics to operate a stiff slide, but there's nothing apart from extensive gunsmithing which is going to make it possible for that person to deal with the heavy trigger of the revolver. Even with expert gunsmithing, there is a certain percentage of the public which simply can't deal with a revolver's trigger. Those are people who should really be looking at an autoloader. (Yes, I know this is a radical position to take, but it's something I firmly believe.)

The revolver's greatest weakness is capacity. The Glock 26 carries more than twice the ammunition of the Smith & Wesson 642.

That same lack of strength also becomes an issue with recoil control. The revolver lacks the recoil-absorbing springs and slide of the autoloader, and doesn't have the grip tang (or 'beavertail') which makes muzzle flip easier to control. The result is that the revolver recoils harder, and the muzzle flips more, than an equivalent autoloader. The revolver's bore height above the hand is also higher than most autoloaders, which only makes the problem worse. Someone who is sufficiently strong but simply recoil sensitive may also want to choose an auto over a revolver.

The most common complaint about the revolver is its ammunition capacity. The average revolver carries five or six rounds, where even tiny autos have 8- or 10-round capacities - and sometimes much more. The revolver's capacity pretty much matches statistical averages of defensive encounters, and there are very few reports of anyone being injured or killed because their revolver didn't carry enough bullets, but that shouldn't keep us from acknowledging reality.

The reality is that the revolver shooter needs to understand and accept that running his or her revolver dry is a very real possibility, and to train for that by getting very good at reloading the gun. I'll get into that in another chapter.

The revolver isn't an outdated relic, but it's not always the perfect answer either. Knowing the gun's limitations, accepting them and working within them is the best way to be truly prepared to use it.

Chapter 3

TRIGGER CONTROL
THE KEY TO SHOOTING

Don't cock a double action revolver - for defensive purposes, there's just no need to do so.

A s I'm fond of saying, the revolver is the easiest gun in the world to shoot - but the most difficult gun in the world to shoot well. Mastering that long and heavy trigger is key to putting your shots where you want them to go, and I've found by far the biggest determinant to precision revolver shooting isn't the sight picture - it's trigger control.

DON'T COCK THAT REVOLVER!

Before getting into the mechanics of the double action trigger, I'd like to suggest that the only way to become good with the double action revolver is to always shoot in double action. This might seem ridiculously self-evident, but I've observed that people tend to take the easy way out when it's available. Shooting in double action is hard, and many people reach a point where they're not getting the hits they need in double action. They take the easy way out and simply thumb-cock the gun for a nice, light single action release. That, I believe, is counterproductive to mastering the double action.

Forgive me if you've heard this story before, but back when I first started shooting the revolver my handgun experience was almost exclusively with single-action autoloaders. I'd picked up a revolver on the cheap and decided to use it in a Bianchi Cup-style NRA Action Pistol Match.

On the first several stages I'd been holding my own; not up to what I could do with my tuned autoloaders, but I wasn't at the back of the pack either. When I got to the falling plates stage, shooting eight-inch round steel knock-down targets at 10, 15, 20 and 25 yards, I failed miserably even at the closest distance. I resorted to thumb-cocking the gun to single action for the rest of the stage, causing one smart-aleck in the pack to yell "Hey, Grant, I've got a gun that cocks itself!"

While this book isn't about competition shooting, the incident serves to illustrate my point: it was because I'd not done my practice in double action

This cocked revolver will require only three pounds of pressure and .020 inch of movement to fire. That's not a good combination in a stressful situation!

Bobbed hammer of double-action-only revolver can't be cocked, even if the owner wants it to be.

that my performance suffered. Had I practiced, forced myself to practice, in the manner in which I was going to use the gun, I'd have been better prepared. After that embarrassment I resigned myself to never shooting in single action again, and it wasn't until I made that decision that I finally got reasonably good at handling the double action revolver.

I contend that you should never thumb-cock a revolver for any defensive shooting purpose, be it practice or an actual incident. Not only is the single action almost universally very light - exactly what you do not want in a trigger when you're trembling and your dexterity and tactile sensation have been reduced - it also has a very short travel to release. Cocking a revolver to single action during an actual attack is a bad idea simply because of the lack of control you'll be to apply to a very sensitive trigger.

It's also very unlikely that a person who is the victim of a surprise criminal attack will even have time to cock the hammer. The duration of these events, measured in a few seconds after the victim recognizes the need to shoot, leaves precious time for a measured, deliberate manipulation. The attacks happen very quickly, and the responsive shots will need to happen quickly as well.

If your revolver isn't going to be used in single action during a defensive engagement, you shouldn't be using it that way when you practice. In later chapters we'll get into the need to practice realistically relative to the expected use, and part of that is using the gun in the same manner you'd expect to when it's 'for real.' That means double action, and it's that on which this book is exclusively focused.

One of the reasons I'm a fan of double-action-only (DAO) revolvers is that they remove the very temptation to cock the hammer - because there's no hammer to cock. I understand the frustration of not being able to make a double action shot while knowing that you could easily do it in single action (I've experienced that in front of an audience!). The DAO revolver removes that temptation and forces you to get better at shooting double action. It forces you to get better at what you're likely to need to do when you're attacked.

If you don't have a DAO revolver, it's going to be up to you to discipline yourself. Shoot the gun only in double action; don't allow yourself the crutch of the single action. This is going to require integrity on your part, but I'll tell you that the personal satisfaction of being able to deliver any given level of precision needed is worth the effort. It also doesn't take all that long to develop that skill, as long as you're not backsliding by allowing yourself the single action crutch.

GRASP: THE FOUNDATION OF TRIGGER CONTROL

Think about this: you're holding a gun that might weigh as little as 12 ounces. The trigger on that gun, if it's as the factory shipped it, may take 13 pounds of pressure (208 ounces) to operate. It's pretty clear that 208 is more than 12, and that extra force needs to be controlled. It's going to take something to keep that 208-ounce force from moving the 12-ounce object around.

That something is your grasp. A grasp that exceeds the 196-ounce difference between the trigger weight and the gun's weight is what you need to stop trigger-induced movement in the gun. That's not going to happen with a weak target-shooting grasp.

Start the grasp with proper hand placement. The web (area between your thumb and forefinger) of the shooting hand should be placed as high as pos-

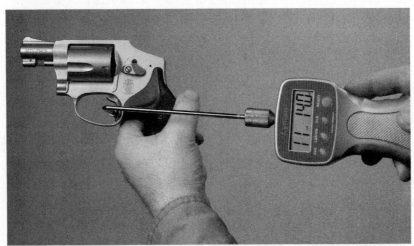

This revolver weighs only 15 ounces but has a trigger weight of nearly 12 pounds. Keeping the muzzle from wandering under that force differential requires proper technique.

Position the web of the hand as high as possible on the gun without going over the top of the frame shoulder.

sible on the grip without spilling over the top of the frame shoulder. This brings the bore line relative to your hand as low as possible, reducing the amount of leverage the gun has, which in turn minimizes recoil and muzzle flip to the greatest degree possible. Bringing the hand higher than this on the grip channels recoil through the edge of the shoulder, increasing the pain level; it's counterproductive.

Remember the safety rules in the first chapter? Unless you're actually shooting, place your trigger finger along the frame just above the trigger and underneath the cylinder and keep it there.

Wrap the rest of your fingers around the grip, making sure that the top of your middle finger is in contact with the underside of the grip behind the triggerguard. (If you're using old-fashioned grips that don't fill in behind the triggerguard, this probably won't be possible. Your control will be severely compromised until proper grips are fitted.)

Unless your grips have finger grooves, the rest of your fingers should be in firm contact with each other. If your grips do have finger grooves, you need to make sure that your fingers don't end up on top of the ridges between the grooves. If they do, your grasp and control over the gun's recoil will be severely compromised, and if the grips are made of a hard material you could even suffer injury.

The tip of the thumb is curled down, much as it would be if you were making a closed fist. This gives you a strong constriction between the web of the

Guns without adequate filling behind the triggerguard, like this old Colt, are more difficult and painful to shoot.

If finger grooves don't precisely match your hand size, fingers can land on top of the ridges, lessening control.

Thumb should be curled down; note open area of grip between fingers and palm.

hand and the middle finger, which acts against the gun's recoil shoulder and keeps the grip from sliding in your hand, both during the trigger stroke and the gun's recoil.

Depending on the size of the grip and your hands, there will probably be a gap that exposes the grip panel between the fingers and heel of your palm. The heel of the support hand is placed in that gap.

The support hand fingers are wrapped around and on top of the shooting hand's fingers. The top of the support hand forefinger should be in contact

The heel of the support hand is placed in the gap.

Wrap the support hand fingers around and on top of the shooting hand fingers.

with the bottom of the trigger guard.

The pad of the support hand thumb should curl down strongly and sit on top of the shooting hand's thumbnail.

Adjust your grip as necessary to get the specified contact points and make a mental note of how everything feels. It's that feeling that you'll want to replicate each time you grasp the gun.

Proper grasp is strong, comfortable and repeatable.

MAXIMUM GRASP PRESSURE IS IMPORTANT

The pressure that you're able to exert in your grasp is what will hold the gun steady when you shoot.

Extend your arms equally straight out as far as you can, putting the gun at arm's length. Now squeeze with both hands as hard as you can, until you start to tremble from the effort. Now ever so slightly release the pressure just enough to stop the trembling, but no more. The resulting pressure will become your normal grasp pressure. (I actually do this little routine at the start of each practice shooting session, just to remind myself how much grip pressure I really need.)

You'll probably find that the resulting pressure is much more than you would otherwise exert without doing this drill. It's the amount you need to apply every time you achieve your shooting grasp. Remember what that feels like and from now on, anytime you extend the gun to fire a shot, make sure that you are exerting that level of pressure.

You'll find that with occasional practice your muscles will rapidly develop from this isometric exercise. The strength of your grasp will increase and you'll have increasing control over your revolver. You'll never get there, however, if you don't start now.

Some people's hands are large enough to encounter interference between trigger finger and thumb. Switching to thumb-on-knuckle grasp solves the issue, but may result in slight loss of control.

GRASP VARIATIONS

Sometimes there is a severe mismatch between the grip size and a shooter's large hand size. This causes the support hand thumb to be so far forward that it interferes with the trigger finger as it comes back.

In these cases simply moving the support thumb up to the knuckle of the shooting hand thumb is enough to give a clear path for the trigger finger. One caution, however - this can result in a slight loss of control unless the shooter is careful to clamp down with the support thumb.

TRIGGER FINGER PLACEMENT

The trigger finger must apply a great deal of force to move the trigger against the spring pressure of the gun's lockwork. In a stock revolver this is often as much as 12 or 13 pounds, and certain guns will weigh in at nearly 15 pounds! To make trigger movement smooth, predictable and repeatable against that amount of weight, it's necessary to take full advantage of finger leverage.

Maximum leverage (and full movement of the trigger finger) is best

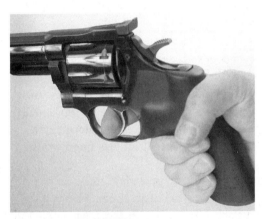

achieved by putting the first (distal interphalangeal) joint of the trigger finger on the trigger face. This gives maximum mechanical advantage and allows for better control of the trigger, as the finger doesn't tire as quickly and movement is smoother.

At one time it was commonly taught to place the pad of the finger on the trigger face. This was necessitated by the wide, serrated 'target' triggers which were then common. While there are still a few prominent shooters who champion this method, the majority of shooters and trainers have long-since transitioned to using the distal joint position because of its clear advantages for the overwhelming majority

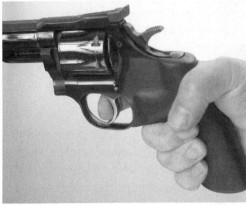

Old technique of finger pad on trigger gives less leverage than modern recommendation of first joint on trigger.

of shooters. Gun manufacturers, too, have responded by making their triggers narrower and without any grooves; this makes it easier to use the more efficient distal joint position.

TRIGGER MANIPULATION AND CONTROL

Once the hand has been properly placed, the grasp pressure has been adjusted to its maximum, and the trigger finger is contacting the trigger properly, trigger manipulation becomes much easier.

Manipulating the double action trigger is much like mastering the stroke in golf. In fact, I use the term stroke to describe the action of operating the trigger because I believe it conveys a much better sense of the movements involved.

Like golf, where there is the swing and the follow-through, the double action trigger has two parts: a compression and a release. Compression is the act of bringing the trigger back against the action's spring pressure, which cocks and then drops the hammer to fire the round. Release is the act of returning the trigger to its forward (rest) position. Both parts are equally important.

COMPRESSION

Trigger compression must be smooth and consistent to avoid steering the gun and throwing the shot off. Once the decision to fire has been made, the trigger is compressed smoothly, evenly and straight back. The compression should be consistent in speed, neither slowing down nor speeding up, and the trigger should be in constant motion until the gun fires. Don't stop or even slow down once the compression has started; keep the trigger finger moving until the gun fires.

Part of the reason for doing this is to keep constant any forces that might cause deviation. Constant, predictable forces are easier to control than those which continually and/or unpredictably change. I've observed that the student who alters the rate of trigger compression will often have a muzzle that wanders excessively. The cause is usually an insufficiently strong grasp, one which doesn't give a solid feeling of control over the revolver. If you find yourself slowing your trigger compression as ignition nears, try increasing your grasp pressure; I've found that it cures the issue most of the time, as it did with me.

RELEASE

The trigger release begins immediately after the hammer falls and the round ignites. The long trigger travel of the revolver delays the firing of the next round unless the trigger is kept in constant motion. This means starting the release without a pause.

The trigger finger simply reduces the amount of pressure it applies to the trigger to the minimum amount necessary to keep in contact as the trigger is allowed to return forward. Your trigger finger should always remain in contact with the trigger as it returns, but only enough so that you can feel the trigger reset; any resistance will simply slow the trigger's movement and may cause you to start another compression before the lockwork has reset. This can result in a temporary jam. Maintain just enough contact so that you can feel the trigger stop, at which point it is completely reset and you can fire the next shot if necessary.

The release should be done at the same speed as the compression. Like the compression, the speed should not vary during the trigger's return movement.

It is also vitally important to pay close attention to your grasp pressure during the return. It's common for the fingers of the hand to relax in sympathy with the relaxing trigger finger, and if that happens the muzzle will surely drift off alignment with the target and likely throw the shot slightly off. On the next shot the grasp needs to be tightened again, which tends to pull the muzzle down and to one side as the trigger is being compressed. The result is a see-sawing of the muzzle, often referred to as "milking" by seasoned instructors. Paying close attention to grasp pressure in practice - first establishing proper pressure as described previously then maintaining that pressure - goes a long way to mastering the long, heavy double action trigger.

FINGER MOVEMENT ON THE TRIGGER

Did I say "on" the trigger? Yes, I did. If you were to diagram the operation of both your trigger and your finger, you'd notice a similarity: both rotate around a pivot point, and both travel in a semicircular path. Neither travels in a straight line.

When operating a trigger, your finger hinges at both the proximal and distal interphalangeal joints, with most of the rotation happening at the latter. The tip of the finger therefore makes an arc (with a slightly decreasing radius, for the geometry purists in the audience) on a horizontal plane. The trigger pivots too, on a pin inside the frame, and the tip of the trigger also travels in an arc (this one is semicircular.)

The arcs of the trigger and your finger are at a right angle to each other. This may not seem like much of a concern, but unless you understand what's happening, you'll do the one thing that most people do to mess up their trigger stroke: you'll 'hang onto' the trigger.

That's because the trigger is traveling up and away from your finger, while your finger is traveling in toward your palm. The result is that the trigger always feels like it's trying to slip away from the finger, and the finger feels like it's going to fall off of the trigger.

When this happens, most people strongly curve the tip of their finger inward in at attempt to hang on to the trigger. This action tends to pull the muzzle down and leads to steering the gun to one side - which side depends on how the gun fits the hand.

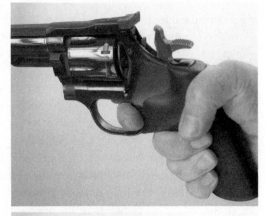

This is why so many people try to stage the trigger - stopping to regroup near the point of ignition - by using the tip of the trigger finger to contact the frame. The finger has curled itself inward in an attempt to diminish the lack of control feeling, which causes the tip to hit the frame. Most people take that as a sign to pause slightly, re-align their sights and then finish off the shot. In a defensive shooting situation there isn't time, or fine tactile function, to allow this to happen.

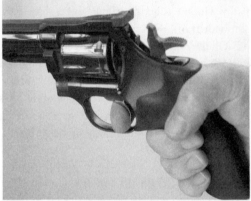

Common issue is trying to hang onto the trigger, curling finger and hitting frame. Letting finger slide on trigger keeps finger from curling, making manipulation easier.

It's far better to solve the problem rather than apply the band-aid of the staged trigger.

The interaction of the trigger and finger arcs means that the finger feels like it wants to slide downward and across the trigger face. Let it! Don't try to hang onto the trigger to keep the finger in one place; let the finger slide naturally across and down the trigger face as it strokes the trigger. The result will be far less muzzle deviation, especially at speed.

This isn't easy to do for some folks. If you've been shooting your revolver with that strongly curled finger, or worse yet by staging the trigger, you're going to have a hard habit to break. Doing so, however, will make you a better double action shooter.

This is one place where dry-fire comes in handy, because it allows you to feel how the finger slides on the face of the trigger. It's not a lot of movement, mind you, but you should be able to feel that slight sliding effect. If you can, it means that you're doing it right.

PUTTING IT TOGETHER

The trigger stroke, except for the direction reversal, should look like a single continuous movement. The goal is to keep the muzzle aligned on target during the stroke - both in compression and release. Compared to an auto-loader, the revolver trigger takes much longer to reset; if you expect to be able to shoot quickly and accurately it's necessary to start the trigger return as the cartridge ignites, and the only way to do that without moving the muzzle off target is to practice making the return as stable as the compression.

For this reason, I recommend practicing the stroke, focusing on trigger return, until the muzzle alignment (as shown by the sights) does not vary during any phase of the stroke. In days past it was a common technique to balance a coin on the front sight and practice the trigger stroke until the coin did not move regardless of which direction the trigger was going. The drill serves to illustrate both what's required and that it's possible to achieve.

A WORD ABOUT TRIGGER FACES

As I mentioned previously, in the 'good old days' double action triggers were typically serrated or grooved. This was to allow the pad of the finger to operate the trigger when it was cocked to single action, as double action shooting wasn't taken all that seriously. It was actually believed by many old-timers that you couldn't hit anything past 'belly-to-belly' distance in double action.

Colt tended to have narrow grooved triggers, while Smith & Wesson had much wider triggers - and had options for extra-wide target triggers. (There were companies which made 'trigger shoes' for Colt revolvers to give them the same trigger width as the Smith & Wessons; some of those shoes were so wide that they extended past the coverage of the triggerguard, which in turn required holsters which didn't cover the trigger.)

Those serrated triggers made double action shooting more difficult because they made it impossible for the finger to slide properly across the trigger face. In recent years revolver manufacturers have figured out that double action shooting technique has changed and now ship revolvers with smooth-faced triggers.

Even if the trigger has a smooth face it may still have very sharp edges that inhibit proper finger movement just as surely as the grooves of yesteryear did. If your revolver has a grooved/serrated trigger, or has sharp edges, a gunsmith can easily round and polish the face of the trigger for you. Your trigger finger will thank you, and your double action shooting will improve.

THOUGHTS ON DRY FIRE PRACTICE

While some may scoff at this, I'm generally not an advocate of extensive dry fire practice for defensive shooting. That isn't to say that it's completely useless, though, because some - of the right kind and in the right proportion - can be helpful in developing proper trigger control.

I've found that dry firing's best benefit is in mastering the release portion of the trigger stroke, and secondly to developing the proper compression. Why do I place them in that order? Because practicing a smooth release is quite difficult with live ammunition; the recoil of the gun masks the trigger reset. You're still resetting the trigger, but the effects of recoil make it impossible to really feel that reset. That recoil also interferes with your ability to judge if you're correctly maintaining your grasp pressure.

Dry firing allows you to divorce the act from the recoil and lets you feel what a proper release is really like. Dry fire also makes it easy to feel grasp strength and if you're maintaining it consistently. Doing these things in dry fire - proper smooth release and consistent grasp pressure during release - will make a huge difference in live fire control.

If you're anything like me, you'll find that when you pay attention to the release in dry fire the compression almost takes care of itself. That's not strictly true, of course, but I've found that mastering the compression portion doesn't benefit quite as much from dry fire. This is probably due to the fact that the compression happens before the shot breaks and isn't masked by the recoil, where he release happens as and just after the round is ignited.

HOW MUCH TO DRY FIRE?

I recommend doing just enough dry fire practice at home that you develop the ability to maintain a perfect sight alignment for the full stroke of the trigger - compression and release - 100% of the time. Once you've achieved that, I maintain that further dry fire in isolation is of little value. That doesn't mean dry fire is completely useless, only that it needs to be done at a different time and place.

I've found that once you've actually fixed in your mind what proper trigger control feels like, any further dry firing is best done at the range just before live fire. In my experience, this immediate transition from the lessons of dry fire to the application of those lessons in live fire provides far more benefit than endlessly dry firing off the range.

I suggest that, when you go to the range, you start by doing a few dry fire repetitions, maybe a cylinder's worth or so, which will be an immense help in fixing in your mind exactly what your hands should be doing. Immediately switching to live fire allows you to transfer the skills to actual shooting. My students have often found that doing so makes both their dry fire and live fire sessions much more productive.

Chapter 4

RELOADING THE REVOLVER

If you're going to use a revolver as a defensive tool you need to acknowledge that you may be more likely to need a rapid reload than you would if using an autoloader. Though I've not unearthed any cases of revolver shooters being injured or killed because their gun had insufficient capacity, it's not outside the realm of plausibility that five or six rounds could prove inadequate - particularly in this day of multiple-assailant attacks. This lack of capacity is one if the revolver's few weaknesses, but luckily it's one that can be addressed through proper technique.

MINIMIZING RELIANCE ON FINE MOTOR SKILLS

The revolver is a difficult arm to reload under the best of conditions. A number of things need to be done in sequence to achieve an efficient reload, and all of them require a certain amount of dexterity and tactile sensation - the very things that are diminished during the body's reaction to a lethal threat.

It's in our interest, then, to adopt a reload technique that minimizes that reliance on fine dexterity.

Note that I said minimizes, not eliminates. We can't get around the fact that we have to interface with the mechanism. Some trainers use that as an excuse to promote techniques that are extremely dexterity-intensive, maintaining that because you have to manipulate the cylinder release you might as well resign yourself to doing everything in ways that demand fine muscle control.

The fact is that we need to use the cylinder release; there's just no other way to get the cylinder open and cleared for the reload. There are other parts of the reload sequence, however, where we do have the choice of techniques that are somewhat less reliant on fine motor skills.

The ultimate in efficiency would be to make the entire process of reloading as failure-proof as possible. Of course that's not possible, simply because

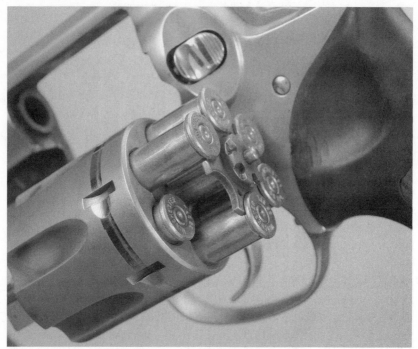

A case caught under the extractor is usually caused by poor reload technique, and wastes any time that may have been saved by trying to go faster.

revolvers just aren't designed that way. However, saying that because we must use fine motor skills in one case means that we should use them in another is a cop-out; we should always strive to make all techniques, including the reload, as resistant to failure as possible. That means reducing to the greatest degree the reliance on fine motor skills wherever possible.

Lack of dexterity isn't the only issue that interferes with the reload, however. An improper reloading technique can actually jam the revolver, in some cases so severely that the only way to clear it is the use of a tool and some time. These are exactly the things that are in short supply during an attack, so it behooves you to learn a technique that reduces as much as possible the chances of that happening.

The reload procedure I recommend does both of those things: reduces the reliance on fine motor skills and reduces the chances of a reloading-related failure to the greatest degree. It also works well with the body's natural reactions and capabilities, making it ideal for the chaos which accompanies a criminal attack. We'll cover that more in depth in Section Two.

There are many different ways to reload the revolver, and some very respected trainers have reasons for advocating their pet methods, but I believe what follows is the most efficient method for dealing with the sudden realization that you have no more bullets in your wheelgun. I also believe that I can

How would you switch your hands on a soccer ball? Just rotate your forearms! This is the basis for the Universal Revolver Reload.

help you understand why it's the most efficient.

(I'll also refer you to the chapter on efficiency in Section Two for a full discussion of the underlying concept - and why it's not the same as speed.)

THE UNIVERSAL REVOLVER RELOAD

This has come to be called the "universal revolver reload" (URR), because it works under the greatest range of conditions and works identically whether it's used with a Colt, Smith & Wesson, Taurus or Ruger revolver.

The basis of the URR is a common, large-muscle-group motor movement, one you've no doubt done many times in your life. Pretend you're holding a basketball in your hands, left hand on the bottom and right hand on the top. How do you reverse the position of your hands without removing them from the ball?

Simple - you just rotate your wrists and let the ball rotate in your hands. It's a simple, gross motor movement primarily involving the large muscles of the forearm. This simple, intuitive action is the basis of the Universal Revolver Reload.

The URR uses the weak (left) hand to simply hold the cylinder, while the more dexterous strong hand performs the tasks that require fine motor control.

Which hand to do what?

There are those who suggest that it's more efficient to keep the revolver in the shooting hand while reloading, largely because it's ever so slightly faster. Faster it may (or may not) be, but it certainly ignores anatomy (and the very real effects of the body's natural reactions in a lethal encounter; more about that later).

If you're like most people you have a strong hand and a weak hand, and your weak hand is probably significantly less able to do precise work than your strong hand. (Even those whose hands are very close in ability find that when they need a high level of precision or dexterity, they use one hand in preference to the other.) We also know that fine motor control degrades under stress, and asking your weak hand to do a fine task under trying conditions is probably not the best way to get it done efficiently.

Relegating the most capable hand to merely cradling the empty gun while performing the most delicate parts of the operation with the hand least suited to doing them is probably not a recipe for success.

I believe a good defensive reload technique must use the strongest, most experienced hand to do the hardest task: getting fresh rounds into their chambers. Relegating the most capable hand to merely cradling the empty gun while performing the most delicate parts of the operation with the hand least suited to doing them is probably not a recipe for success.

This is why the universal revolver reload has the weak hand do the simple tasks while the strong hand does the complex ones.

As you recognize the need to reload, take your finger off the trigger and lay it on the frame of the revolver, above the trigger. Your eyes should remain on the threat; you should practice reloading the revolver without needing to watch the process.

When it's time to reload, take your finger off the trigger and lay it on the frame of the revolver, above the trigger.

Move your support hand forward so your thumb is on the frame in front of the cylinder and your two middle fingers are touching the cylinder on the opposite side.

Extend your shooting hand thumb straight forward toward the muzzle, and allow the gun to rotate to the right.

As you bring the gun back toward your body for better strength and control, move your left (support) hand forward so that your thumb is on the frame in front of the cylinder, and your two middle fingers are touching the cylinder on the opposite side.

At the same time simply extend your shooting hand thumb straight forward toward the muzzle. Regardless of whether you have a Colt, Ruger or Smith & Wesson, simply point your thumb forward. Just as you did with the imaginary basketball, you're going to use your wrists and forearms to rotate the gun to the right. Allow the gun to rotate in your grasp.

As the muzzle rotates toward a vertical position, the cylinder release and your thumb will make contact, and as the gun continues to rotate it will push the release into your relatively stationary thumb. This will result in the latch being depressed without a lot of effort on your part. Whether you have a Colt, Smith & Wesson or Ruger doesn't matter - just let the gun rotate the release button into your thumb. A Smith & Wesson will release very early in the rotation, a Ruger a little later, and a Colt very late. No matter when that happens, let the gun do the work for you.

As the cylinder unlatches, the fingers of your left hand will naturally apply pressure against the movement of the gun to open the cylinder. Remember: it's the movement of the gun against your fingers that does the work. As the muzzle comes to the vertical position, just let the gun rotate around the middle fingers of your left hand thus pushing the cylinder fully open. Grasp the cylinder between your thumb and fingers to immobilize it, and remove your right hand from the grip.

Immobilizing the cylinder this way makes it very difficult to bend the crane (the arm on which the cylinder rotates) when ejecting the cases or inserting

The movement of the gun against your fingers does the work. As the muzzle comes to the vertical position, let the gun rotate around the middle fingers of your left hand, pushing the cylinder fully open.

Grasp the cylinder with the fingers and thumb of the support hand, and remove your right hand from the grip.

a push-to-release speedloader. It also keeps the cylinder from rotating when using the twist-to-release style of speedloader.

Up to this point you've used primarily large muscle groups and gross motor movements, which are very resistant to degradation during the body's natural response to a threat. Those natural reactions are the very reason this reloading method exists.

Flatten your right hand and swiftly strike the ejector rod one time with your palm. This accelerates the brass and tends to throw it clear of the cylin-

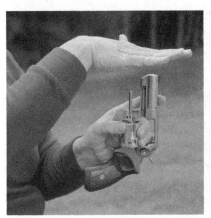

Strike the ejector rod one time with your palm. Velocity is more important than force, and it's important that you only strike the ejector rod one time only.

der, even with short ejector rods. Velocity is more important than force, and it's important that you only strike the ejector rod one time. If there are any cases which fail to clear the cylinder, multiple ejections will not clear them but will significantly raise the risk of a case-under-extractor jam. The combination of the cylinder pointing at the ground, the quick extractor strike, and striking only once virtually eliminates the risk of such a jam. (If for some reason there are cases that don't clear, you can pick them out later without danger of a jam.)

This action makes use of proprioception, which is the body's natural ability to locate its limbs in free space. Proprioception is why we can walk without watching our feet; it's why we can touch our noses with our fingers when our eyes are closed; it's why we can tie an apron behind our back. It's as reliable a sense as we have. To eject the casings, all you have to do is bring your hands together; since the ejector rod is in the middle of the hand that's holding the cylinder, when your hands come together the rod will be depressed; you can't help but do it! If you were holding the gun any other way you'd need to figure out a method of locating the ejector rod so you could operate it. This way, all you have to do is bring your hands together and the job is done.

Rotate the muzzle toward the ground, bringing the gun down to the mid-abdominal level. Your elbow should be tight into your side; if you were to move suddenly, the gun should stay immobile relative to your abdomen.

As the muzzle comes down, your right hand simultaneously retrieves your ammunition - speedloader, SpeedStrip or loose rounds. Insert the rounds into the cylinder; proprioception again works in your favor, allowing you to get

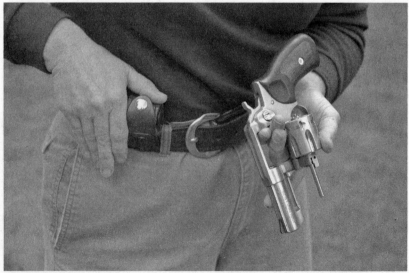

Rotate the muzzle toward the ground, keeping your support-arm elbow tight to your side, simultaneously retrieving your ammunition with your right hand.

Insert the rounds into the cylinder.

the fresh ammunition to the cylinder without needing to look. Again, all you need to do is bring your hands together and the ammunition will contact the cylinder; this would not be the case if you that cylinder wasn't being held in your palm.

To close the cylinder, simply roll your hands toward each other as if you were closing a book. The revolver is now recharged; all you need to do is bring your support hand back and re-establish a good shooting grip.

Remember to let the gun do the work by letting it rotate in your hands. You

Once the rounds are in the cylinder, reestablish your firing grasp.

don't have to think about searching for the release catch or forcibly pushing the cylinder open or stick your fingers into the frame window - the natural movement of the gun in your hands will do that for you.

SPEEDLOADER TECHNIQUE

The most efficient way to recharge your revolver is to use a speedloader. The speedloader inserts all rounds into the cylinder simultaneously and greatly reduces the fiddling necessary to get bullet noses started into their chambers.

The speedloader really comes into its own when paired with the Universal Revolver Reload. With one hand holding the cylinder and the other handling the speedloader you can take advantage of proprioception; all you need to do is to bring your hands together and the speedloader will be right on top of the cylinder where it needs to be. Reloading in the dark or while keeping your eyes on your threat is more efficiently accomplished with the speedloader than with any other method.

Like anything else, there is a technique to using the speedloader. Poor speedloader technique can slow the reload significantly. Here's what I've found to be the best way to use one.

When you retrieve your speedloader, it's important to grasp it by the body, and ideally so that your fingers align with and extend just past the bullet noses. This slightly enhances the effect of proprioception and makes it easier to handle the speedloader. If you don't get it exactly right, don't worry; the technique won't fail if your fingers aren't in exactly the right place. The most

When retrieving the speedloader, the most important thing is to grasp it by the body, not by the knob.

As you bring the hand with the speedloader toward the one that is holding the cylinder, the speedloader will naturally end up over the chambers.

important thing is to grasp the speedloader by the body, not by the knob!

As you bring the hand with the speedloader toward the one that is holding the cylinder, proprioception ensures that the speedloader will naturally end up over the chambers. Just bring your hands together.

(Some trainers advise, and I used to teach, that the tips of your fingers can make contact with the edge of the cylinder to

As the bullet noses come into contact with the cylinder, simply jiggle the speedloader by twisting it very slightly and very quickly clockwise and counter-clockwise.

help align the rounds with the chambers. I've found that's not necessarily true, particularly if your initial grasp of the speedloader doesn't leave your fingertips in front of the bullet noses. Instead, I now teach to simply bring your hands together - the speedloader will be in just the right position automatically.)

Once rounds have dropped into the chambers, release them from the speedloader.

Sometimes you'll get lucky and the bullet noses happen to line up with the chambers; other times they'll line up on the metal between the chambers. The solution is simple: as the bullet noses come into contact with the cylinder, simply jiggle the speedloader by twisting it very slightly and very quickly clockwise and counterclockwise. The bullets will drop into the chambers without further work on your part. (This is a fine motor skill, which validates my insistence on using your most dexterous hand to do the job.)

After the rounds have dropped into the chambers, release them by whatever method your speedloader

With an HKS or similar speedloader, twist the knob to release the rounds.

Pull the speedloader straight back to make sure all of the rounds have cleared . . .

brand requires. If you're using a Safariland or SL Variant, simply push the body of the speedloader toward the cylinder and the rounds will release.

If your speedloader is an HKS or similar design, insert the rounds into the cylinder, then grab the knob and twist it to release the rounds.

As the rounds drop from the speedloader, pull it straight back out to make sure all of the rounds have cleared, then drop it over the side of the gun. This eliminates another failure point of the reload procedure: rounds binding in the loader.

It's not uncommon to have the speedloader tilt just a bit and cause a round or two to bind inside the loader. When this happens the round(s) don't clear the loader, and if you attempt to close the cylinder you'll trap that round(s) and the speedloader against the frame of the gun. You'll then need to open the cylinder, grab the speedloader, shake the round(s) loose and finally finish the reload. Yes, it's time consuming and aggravating, which is why I strive to avoid it by lifting the loader and allowing the rounds to drop free, then tossing the speedloader away.

. . . then drop it over the side of the gun.

Tilting the speedloader just a bit can cause a round or two to bind inside the loader.

SPEEDLOADER RECOMMENDATIONS

The two most common and widely available speedloaders on the market are the Safariland, which use a push-to-release mechanism, and the HKS, which releases by turning a knob. (There are other examples of each style, such as the push-type SL Variant and the turn-type Five Star, but Safariland and HKS are by far the most readily available. They're the least expensive in their respective categories as well.)

In general I much prefer the Safariland, simply because they're more intuitive in use. You're already grasping the speedloader by its body and pushing the rounds into the cylinder; releasing the rounds from the Safariland is a simple continuation of that movement. The HKS style, on the other hand, requires you to release your grasp of the body, find the knob and grab it, then twist it in the proper direction to allow the rounds to drop into the cylinder. I don't consider that as intuitive as simply continuing pushing the way you're already pushing.

I've also found that the Safariland speedloaders, when properly loaded, are more secure. They're less likely to accidentally release in a pocket or when dropped.

Author feels Safariland speedloader on left is more intuitive in use and more secure than HKS on right.

LOADING THE SAFARILANDS

Properly loaded, I've never had a Safariland Comp I or Comp II speed-loader accidentally release - even when purposely dropped and kicked into a concrete wall, a demonstration which I've done many times. Some shooters, however, have reported exactly the opposite. The difference between my experience and everyone else's? How the things are loaded.

If you follow Safariland's loading instructions, accidental release is far more likely.

I've learned the hard way that if you follow Safariland's loading instructions accidental release is far more likely. Safariland says to put the rounds into the speedloader, then invert the assembly onto something like a table so that the bullet noses are resting on a hard surface. The speedloader's knob is then pushed in and turned to lock in the rounds. This is where the problem occurs.

Normal manufacturing tolerances for ammunition allow for a certain variance in bullet length and in the overall length of loaded rounds. It's possible to get a round in which the bullet is slightly shorter than normal, and/or where the round itself has an overall length that's on the short side of acceptable. It's also possible to get the opposite - a round that is slightly long but still 'in spec.'

When those two rounds are inserted into the same speedloader and then that speedloader is inverted onto a flat surface, the longer rounds hold the speedloader body a little high. The shorter rounds aren't pushed up far enough to completely engage the locking cam around their rims and aren't positively retained. When that speedloader is jostled just right, the rounds that aren't held solidly will drop loose. (Sometimes that results in the complete emptying of the loader.)

Instead of doing that, I recommend that you hold the loader so that it's pointing up and insert the rounds with the bullets pointing skyward. As you push in and turn the locking knob, jiggle the whole thing slightly. This allows the rounds to make positive contact with the body of the loader and allows them to work securely under the extractor. If any one round doesn't lock securely you can feel it instantly; releasing the lock and relocking fixes the problem.

This technique ensures that the heads of the cartridges are positively seated in the speedloader base, giving the locking mechanism proper access to the rims. In nearly two decades of loading Safariland speedloaders in this manner, I've yet to experience an accidental release, even when intentionally trying to get it to happen.

SPEEDSTRIP TECHNIQUE

The SpeedStrip, Tuffstrip and other similar products are rubber strips that hold rounds by their rims. (SpeedStrip, like Kleenex, is a brand name that's

To prevent accidental release of the rounds, hold the loader so that it's pointing up and insert the rounds with the bullets pointing skyward.

Carry only four rounds in the strip, leaving a blank space in the middle to use as a handling tab.

come to be used to refer to any such devices. It's actually a registered trademark of Bianchi International.) They hold the rounds in a row, which makes them very flat and convenient to carry.

Since they are only usable to insert two rounds at a time, however, they're much slower and more dependent on fine motor skills than are speedloaders. To help compensate for their shortcomings, I have a specific way of configuring and using them.

First, I recommend that

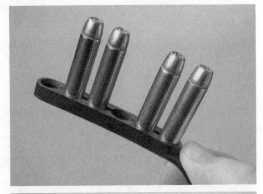

No matter how you wind up grabbing the strip, you'll have a way to hang onto it.

Push the rounds in, then simply 'peel' the strip off the case heads, allowing them to drop into the cylinder.

Do the same with the other two rounds.

you carry only four rounds in your strips. Start at the tab end and load two rounds, leave one blank space, and load two more rounds leaving a leftover space at the other end. This provides a handling tab at each end and one in the middle.

No matter how you wind up grabbing the strip, you'll have a way to hang onto it and sufficient space to get your fingers in to manipulate the rounds as they go into the cylinder. This makes a big difference when peeling the strip off of the rounds in the chambers.

Retrieve the strip (I prefer a back pocket or the watch pocket of a pair of jeans) and insert two rounds into adjacent chambers. Again, proprioception is your friend: simply bring the ammo toward the palm of the hand holding the cylinder, wiggle slightly to get the bullet noses started into the chambers, and push the rounds in. Then simply 'peel' the strip off the case heads, allowing them to drop the rest of the way into the cylinder.

If time permits, do the same with the other two rounds. I don't shift the strip in my hand; I simply use the heel of my palm to push them into the chambers and then peel off the strip.

Now drop the strip and close the cylinder. Back in business!

LEFT HAND RELOADING

Most of my left handed students have found the following to be workable. Like the right handed URR, it uses the same principles of proprioception, gross motor movements wherever possible, and using the most experienced and dexterous hand to do the important task of getting the rounds into the cylinder.

Bring the right hand forward so that the cylinder can be pinched between

Pinch the cylinder between the thumb and fore and middle fingers.

Operate the cylinder release with the forefinger of the left hand.

The cylinder is held firmly with the thumb and fingers of the right hand.

the thumb, fore and middle fingers.

Using the forefinger of the left hand, operate the cylinder release. (I've found it helpful to use the side of my forefinger to do so, supported where necessary by the left thumb on the opposite side of the frame.) This is much easier with Ruger revolvers than either Colt or Smith & Wesson.

Strike the ejector rod only once.

Insert the spare ammunition.

As the cylinder unlatches, rotate the frame around the right thumb so that the cylinder window ends up at the base of the thumb. The cylinder should be held firmly immobilized between the thumb and fingers of the right hand.

Strike the ejector rod swiftly with the left palm, once only.

Rotate the muzzle toward the ground, retrieve the spare ammunition with the left hand and insert into the cylinder.

Pull the right thumb out of the frame and close the cylinder.

Return to two-handed grip.

Re-establish a firing grip; pull the right thumb out of the frame, and close the cylinder with the fingers.

Go back to a two-handed grip.

Like the right-handed universal revolver reload, this method is designed to avoid the critical stall points in the reload process and make the reload more efficient in critical situations.

PRACTICING THE RELOAD

There are a couple of key points when practicing the revolver reload. First, resist the urge to speed the reload up by taking shortcuts. I teach a completely different reloading technique to competition shooters, where the possibility of a reloading failure doesn't offset a small speed advantage. (More precisely, the speed advantage offsets the small chance of a failed reload process.) In a defensive situation, however, the tenths of a second saved are not worth a botched reload.

> I lost an important match one day because I was using a competition reloading technique, one that was optimized for speed above reliability. I'd done it thousands of times, but on this one occasion I was within striking distance of a very good shooter and going into a stage where I knew a particular shooting ability would give me an insurmountable lead. When my super-fast reload left me with a case under the extractor, I ended up a full sixty points behind the guy! That event caused me to understand that if it had happened in the middle of a defensive shooting I might not survive. Resist the urge to take shortcuts that reduce the reliability of the process.

Second, practice in context. We'll talk more about this concept in Section Two, but right now it's sufficient to suggest that you practice the reload in live fire as much as possible. I used to practice my reloads dry - at home using realistically weighted dummy rounds - in order to prepare for competition. I'll bet I did ten thousand repetitions to become as fast as I could.

The problem was that I didn't link that athletic skill with the recognition of the need to reload, and when I shot in a match it would take me a few fractions of a second to go from the realization that I was out of ammunition to the actual act of the reload. The stimulus of the suddenly empty gun was missing in my dry runs. When I switched from dry reloads to incorporating as many reloads as possible in live fire, I was finally able to make the necessary link between the stimulus and the response. You'll read a lot more about this concept later; the important thing is to practice reloads in live fire as much as possible.

ONE-HAND RELOADING

Reloading the revolver with one hand is an advanced skill, in the sense that it's not one that has widespread application. The only reason you'd ever want to reload the revolver with one hand is because your other hand is inoperable for some reason.

It's possible that during your response to an attack that you could sustain an injury to your hand that renders it unable to function well enough to participate in the reload process. It's a slim possibility that you'd be injured and you need to reload your revolver, to be sure, but it's plausible that it could happen.

A more likely scenario is one where you've injured your hand or had a recent surgical procedure that has left it unusable for a period of time. Many surgeries, such as the common procedure to correct carpal tunnel syndrome, can and do take one hand out of service for a period of time. This is, I believe, the most rational reason to at least be familiar with these techniques.

Because reloading with one hand isn't what one could call a core skill, I wouldn't recommend spending a lot of time on practice. Running through the procedure once or twice every so often, though, will help you maintain at least a passing acquaintance with the process.

Right hand only

You've fired your last shot and recognized that you need to reload your revolver. Finger off the trigger!

Bring your thumb up to the hammer spur as you would if you were cocking the gun to single action. (If you're using a hammerless gun, put it on the back of the frame where a hammer spur would be.) Bring the gun back to your body and rest the butt of the gun somewhere between the top of your belt and the bottom of your sternum. This is the key to doing an efficient one-hand reload: anchoring the gun to your body. Having the butt contact your body, actually resting there, gives you a solid point around which you can maneuver your hand. This is critical - if the butt of the gun is hanging in free space, it's a lot harder to do the manipulation necessary to complete the reload. WIth the butt anchored, your hand can move anywhere on the gun, wherever it may need to be, without fumbling.

Move your hand up on top of the gun, so that the web of your thumb and forefinger is on the top strap, your thumb is touching the cylinder release, and your fingers are touching the cylinder on the opposite side. You may find that it's necessary to rotate the gun, using the butt as a pivot point, to make this easier to manage.

Operate the cylinder release with your thumb while simultaneously pushing the cylinder open with your fingers. As the cylinder opens, push your fingers into and through the frame opening.

First step: Finger off the trigger!

This is the key to doing an efficient one-hand reload: anchoring the gun to your body.

Move your hand up on top of the gun.

Operate the cylinder release with your thumb while simultaneously pushing the cylinder open with your fingers.

As the cylinder opens, push your fingers into and through the frame opening.

Position your thumb on the ejector rod, then push the ejector rod - swiftly and fully - one time only.

Rotate the gun and insert the muzzle into your waistband.

Check for any un-ejected cases.

Insert your spare ammunition.

Twist your hand around to get an approximate firing grip.

The gun should now be held by the top strap with your fingers wedging the cylinder in the open position. Position your thumb on the ejector rod, and lift the gun free of contact with your body.

Push the ejector rod swiftly and fully, one time only. With a two-hand reload the chances of a case-under-ejector jam increase greatly with each successive ejection, and it's worse with one hand because the ejector isn't being operated at the same velocity. Resist the urge to pump the ejector rod; a healthy shake of the gun as you depress the ejector will help accelerate the casings free of the cylinder.

Rotate the gun so that the muzzle is pointing down and insert the barrel into your waistband. I find it helpful to put my thumb on the barrel, pointing in a parallel direction, to help guide the gun. The cylinder needs to be on the outside of the waistband.

Let go of the gun and sweep your hand over the top of the cylinder, feeling for any un-ejected cases. If you find any, pluck them out and drop them.

Get your spare ammunition, in whatever form you're using, and insert the rounds into the cylinder.

Twist your hand around so that you can get an approximate firing grip on the gun, and pull it free of the waistband.

Twist the gun clockwise into a natural position, bring the cylinder into contact with your waistband, and rotate the gun counter-clockwise to close and latch the cylinder. (Do not flip the cylinder closed - I don't care how many times you've seen it on TV.) You're reloaded and ready to go.

Rotate the gun to close and latch the cylinder.

Left hand only

After your last shot, bring your finger off the trigger and pull the gun back to contact with your body.

Rotate the gun to the left as you bring your hand higher on the backstrap of the grip. Your thumb should be pointing in the general direction of the muzzle and contacting the cylinder.

The side of your forefinger should be contacting the cylinder release. As it operates the release latch, the thumb pushes the cylinder open.

Once the cylinder is open work your hand forward so that you're holding the gun by the topstrap, with your thumb under the barrel and contacting the ejector rod.

Push the ejector rod swiftly and fully, one time only. Remember that the chances of a case-under-ejector jam increase greatly with each successive ejection, so resist the urge to pump the ejector rod. A healthy shake of the gun as you do this will help accelerate the casings free of the cylinder.

Invert the gun and push the muzzle down and into your waistband. The cylinder should be on the outside of the waistband.

Pul the gun back to contact with your body.

Rotate the gun. Thumb should be contacting the cylinder.

Operate the cylinder release with the forefinger, and push the cylinder open with the thumb.

Work your hand forward.

A healthy shake of the gun as you push the ejector rod will help accelerate the casings free of the cylinder.

Invert the gun and insert the muzzle into your waistband.

Check for any cases that failed to eject, then insert your spare ammnition.

Sweep your fingers over the top of the cylinder and feel for cases that failed to eject. Pull out any that you find, retrieve your spare ammunition and insert the rounds into the cylinder.

Get a firing grip on the gun, pulling it out of the waistband.

Re-establish firing grip and pull gun from waistband.

Rotate the gun clockwise, bringing it to your backside.

Close and latch the cylinder.

Twist the gun clockwise so that the cylinder is on the inside, and bring it to the backside.

Rotate the gun to close and latch the cylinder. Again, don't flip the cylinder closed!

IMPORTANT POINTS

Having the gun butt in contact with the body makes it easy to 'walk' the hand over the gun to perform the necessary functions. Without doing that, the gun has to be juggled in the hand, making it more likely that the gun will be dropped. By bringing the butt into contact with the body you stabilize it, making it possible to reach any part of the gun easily. Use that solid contact point to your advantage.

Author's gun position for right-hand-only reload.

Author's gun placement for left-hand-only reload.

When doing a right-hand reload I tend to place the butt on top of my belt. This seems to give me a good anchor without having to push the gun into my belly, and puts it at a natural and easy to manage height and angle.

When doing the left-hand reload, though, I tend to bring it closer to my sternum. The butt seems to nestle in that little hollow at the base of the sternum, which (for me) better suits the different angles that the left hand needs to execute. As you'll learn in later chapters, I'm usually a big proponent of consistency in technique, but in this case I think the deviation is justified by better control and more efficient movement.

Using this method you'll find that even the Dan Wesson revolver, with its cylinder release on the crane in front of the cylinder, is not a problem to reload. I've found that Rugers are the easiest to manage one-handed, largely because operating the cylinder release is an easily performed pinch that is helped by the support by the fingers on either side of the frame. The difference is quite small, however, and may be due more to hand size than anything.

Keep your mind on the task at hand when doing any one-handed manipulation. It's very easy to let a finger stray into the trigger guard when closing the cylinder, which is a condition you want to avoid. Pay attention to where your fingers are at all times and once the cylinder is closed pay careful attention to what your muzzle is covering as you come back onto target.

Chapter 5

AMMUNITION
FOR DEFENSIVE SHOOTING

Your goal when using your revolver in a defensive encounter is to make the bad guy stop doing whatever it is that required you to shoot in the first place. To be clear: you want to stop the threat. Your goal is not to create a fatality, though that is a distinct possibility, but rather to cause the attacker to stop his activity.

MECHANISMS OF STOPPING THE THREAT

A stop can be due to either of two mechanisms: psychological, where the attacker makes the decision that he really doesn't want to persist and longer; and physiological, where the attacker's body involuntarily stops functioning because of the damage that has been inflicted.

Psychological stops

Psychological incapacitation is very unpredictable. There are people who will stop and run when confronted by a well-thrown rock, while others will remain undeterred by Mace, Tasers, and baton hits without so much as flinching. This is particularly true with people who are drunk or on drugs; their sensation of pain is dulled, and very often their intoxication results in antagonistic or psychotic behavior that is resistant to psychological trauma.

Since psychological stops are all in the mind and people's minds vary significantly (especially when intoxicated or otherwise under the influence) you simply cannot count on delivering a jolt to a criminal's psyche reliably enough to cause him (or her) to stop every single time. Instead, you'll need to focus on doing enough physical damage to your attacker to make it impossible for him to continue to function.

125 grain .357 Magnum round on left is light & fast - up to 1450 feet per second. 230 grain .45 ACP round is heavy & slow, clocking in around 850 fps. Both work, but so do many others that fit in between.

Physiological stops

As it happens, a bullet needs to do two critical tasks to deliver a level of physical interdiction that will result in an involuntary shut down:

1) It has to get to something the body finds immediately important, and

2) It has to do rapid and significant disruption to that thing when it arrives.

Either, by itself, simply won't reliably cause the physical damage necessary for incapacitation. If the round fails at either of these tasks, any incapacitation that occurs is probably psychological in nature - which I hope I've convinced you is both unpredictable and unreliable.

Yes, small caliber bullets fail. Guess what?
Large caliber bullets fail, too.

The better the bullet performs those tasks, the faster incapacitation is likely to occur. Note that I said likely. Handgun rounds are underpowered things and the human body is incredibly resilient; that combination means that nothing is ever certain. Your goal should be to stack the deck in your favor by controlling as many variables as possible.

While this may sound like heresy to some, the fact is that within certain limits it doesn't really matter what the caliber is or what the bullet is made of or how fast it travels, as long as it does both of those critical tasks. That's why there seems to be such a wide range of calibers, weights and velocities that work in defensive shootings: there is a pretty big arena in terms of how that job can be done, and that arena contains quite a number of cartridges and bullets.

The reason that the "heavy and slow" and "light and fast" apologists exist is because, generally, both choices just happen do both of the tasks on a fairly regular basis. Arguing about which is the better approach is really quite silly, because when they work it's because they did both tasks. When they fail, it's because they didn't do one (or both) of the tasks.

Here's the reality: yes, small caliber bullets fail. Guess what? Large caliber bullets fail, too. A good friend gave me a first-person account of a battle incident wherein a fellow soldier absorbed several solid torso hits and was still able to jump from his vehicle and get to the side of a country road before finally collapsing. The gun in question? A .50 caliber heavy machine gun. Yes, you read that correctly. Nothing - absolutely nothing - works every single time.

You must understand that when it comes to firearms and the human body, everything and anything can fail. Your job is to choose a caliber and bullet which seem to do those two critical tasks fairly reliably, and understand that there may be times that it just isn't enough. That's why you train and practice.

GETTING TO SOMETHING IMPORTANT

No matter what bullet is used, the person shooting that bullet needs to be capable of putting it on a course that will lead it to something important. Some cartridges are simply more challenging to shoot, particularly when firing the rapid, multiple shots that are necessary in defensive shooting. The first bullet needs to get to something the attacker's body finds immediately important - but so do the second and third and fourth. A cartridge that you can't control in realistic strings of fire is going to be less effective than one that you can.

Once the bullet is fired it has to defeat some obstacles to reach something important. Those obstacles include clothing, skin (which is a lot tougher than you might believe), bone and muscle. It has to penetrate all of those.

Penetration is key

When dealing with conventional solid bullets, the caliber (diameter), weight and shape of the bullet all effect the penetration. All other things being equal, the more pointed the bullet the more it will penetrate; heavier bullets usually result in more penetration as well.

Expanding bullets (softnose or hollowpoint) increase their diameter when they enter the target. The frontal area increases dramatically as the bullet expands and acts something like a parachute, slowing the bullet and reducing penetration. This can be a problem if the penetration is reduced to the point that the bullet fails to have sufficient penetration, so expansion needs to be carefully controlled in order to be useful.

Too much penetration can be as bad as too little. A bullet with excessive penetration can move through the target and endanger innocents behind. This isn't a theoretical issue; there are records of police shootings where people have been hit and killed by bullets which had already penetrated the body of someone else.[7] It's important from both a performance and a safety standpoint to have a bullet which has sufficient penetration, but not an excessive amount.

Some cartridges, when loaded with streamlined, roundnosed bullets, will travel through multiple targets, but when loaded with expanding bullets stop inside the first one. As it turns out, this has major benefits to the second task.

DOING WORK WHEN IT GETS THERE

I often refer to the second task as 'doing work,' because that's exactly what the bullet does. Its work just happens to be doing damage to the target.

The only reason a bullet does anything at all is because of its kinetic (moving) energy, and once it reaches its target the energy in a bullet can only do one of two things: it can be used to inflict damage to the target (work), or it can be wasted beyond the target.

As the bullet travels through the target, it uses its energy to crush or displace the clothing, skin, bone, muscle or organs which it encounters. The amount of energy it uses is highly dependent on its shape; the more streamlined the bullet, the less work it does and the less energy it uses. If the bullet

Expanding bullet uses part of its available energy in mushrooming. Careful ammunition choice ensures that there's enough energy left for proper penetration. (Photo courtesy of Hornady Manufacturing.)

has a flattened shape it needs more energy to get through the target than it does if it has a nice, smooth, round nose.

If the bullet expands in the target, some of its energy is used to deform the bullet itself and the rest is used to push the much larger, flatter profile through the target. In some cases it uses up all its energy trying to get through the target and never makes it out the other side. This is why, as I alluded to above, penetration can be controlled through the use of an expanding bullet.

The advantage of the expanding hollowpoint

The critical aspect of the second task is that, once the bullet gets to something that the body deems immediately important, it impart rapid and significant disruption. This is where the expanding bullet, most commonly the hollowpoint, has a significant advantage: once expanded it presents a much larger frontal area to impact whatever it contacts. That large expanded nose, many times larger in area than the diameter of the bullet, provides a lot more disruption than its non-expanding counterparts. Expanding bullets are therefore more effective and far more desirable.

Since the energy to deform the bullet is supplied by the bullet's movement, there needs to be enough remaining energy after expansion to do the necessary work. This is why I say that the bullet has to create rapid and significant disruption when it arrives; if it gets there but has so little energy left that it is incapable of inflicting necessary damage, then it is nearly as if it had not gotten there to begin with.

Your overriding goal, remember, is to stop the bad guy.

Don't misunderstand: I'm not saying that the wound in such a case isn't serious. It is. But our goal in a defensive shooting is to make the attacker stop what he's doing by compromising his ability to function - and the sooner that happens, the better. The only reliable way to achieve that result is to disrupt an important physiological function. If that doesn't happen quickly, it's possible that the defender - that would be you - could be injured or even killed while waiting for the attacker to cease functioning.

The classic example is a criminal who gets shot with a lowly .22 rimfire. He might still be able to complete his assault even though he might succumb to peritonitis a few days later. That wound certainly isn't trivial, but since it didn't achieve the goal of stopping the criminal before he could harm someone else it has failed. Your overriding goal, remember, is to stop the bad guy.

CHOOSING DEFENSIVE AMMUNITION

Many years of shooting data has shown that the best defensive ammunition is a hollowpoint bullet that expands reliably in the target and penetrates sufficiently to reach vital organs. There may be instances where that choice isn't possible, but for the vast majority of people under the vast majority of circumstances the modern hollowpoint is what's needed.

Since the majority of revolvers used for defensive shooting are chambered in .38 Special or .357 Magnum, it shouldn't be surprising that the majority of ammunition suitable for self defense is in these two cartridges.

In .38 Special, best results seem to come from the mid- to heavy-weight bullets (135 grains to 158 grains) in +P loadings. At this writing, the Speer Gold Dot Hollowpoint (GDHP) +P 135gn is the standout choice. Originally developed for the NYPD for backup and off-duty guns, it's racked up a large number of shootings and has performed extremely well. Most of the modern lightweight revolvers shoot this load to point of aim.

An older load that has a very long track record of good performance is the 158gn +P Lead Semi-Wadcutter Hollowpoint (LSWCHP.) This has been loaded by Winchester, Remington and Federal at various times and has the virtue of being relatively inexpensive and packaged in 50-round boxes. My preference, based on expanded diameter in testing, is Remington, Federal and Winchester - in that order. This load generally shoots to point of aim in older revolvers.

A promising newcomer is the Winchester PDX1 Defender, which is a 130gn +P load. The bullet is a bit lighter than I would like to see, but the PDX1 line in general has proven to be intelligently engineered and has been turning in good performances. It is worth watching to see how it actually does in the field, but I wouldn't feel at all hesitant to load it in my guns if it were available.

The .357 Magnum has long been ruled by the 125gn Semi-Jacketed Hollowpoint (SJHP) loads from the major ammunition makers. This is the load that defined the .357 as a "manstopper" back in the '70s and '80s (though recent analysis of shooting data by experts such as Greg Ellifritz casts doubt on that reputation). The 125gn has a mixed record; when it worked, it worked very well but it sometimes expanded far too quickly, leading to shallow and ineffective wounds.

While I don't recommend anyone carry a Magnum of any type these days, primarily because of the much greater difficulty in controlling the gun in realistic strings of fire, for those who insist I suggest a more modern and slightly heavier bullet. Speer makes their excellent 135gn Gold Dot GDHP in .357, and that would be my pick for its ability to maintain structural integrity in the target.

Once you move away from those calibers, the pickings get very slim. In .327 Magnum, the issue is getting a bullet with sufficient mass to penetrate

The 125 grain hollowpoint on left is usual recommendation in .357 Magnum, but author prefers Speer 135 grain load on right.

deeply enough. The only loads at this writing which hold out promise are both from the Speer Gold Dot line: the 115gn GDHP and the 100gn GDHP, in that order. Keep in mind that there are no defensive shootings of which I'm aware with either of these loads; the recommendation is based on seeing their results in testing.

The .44 Special is an on-again, off-again cartridge. There are times when everyone seems to rediscover this old cartridge and ammunition suddenly becomes widely available, only to disappear as people move on to something else. I've watched this same sequence replay itself several times over the years.

The .44 Magnum is a poor round for self defense, being overly penetrative and difficult to control.

The technical problem with this load is the same as faced by the .38 Special: lack of bullets which both expand reliably and penetrate sufficiently. In addition, there are very few defensive shootings on record, which further complicates matters.

After talking with people who use the .44 Special for hunting, the choice appears to be the 165gn Cor-Bon Self-Defense JHP. This round is currently the only widely available hollowpoint that will exhibit reliable expansion out of a typical four-inch barrel, which makes it the top pick in a rather sparse field.

The .44 Magnum is a poor round for self defense, being overly penetrative and difficult to control for all but the most experienced of handgunners. However, there may be circumstances where a revolver has to do double duty for both hunting and self defense against criminal attack in the field.

In such cases, the first preference would be to use one of the .44 Special rounds listed above. If those aren't available, it's preferable to pick a relatively lightweight (no more than 200 grains) hollowpoint to limit the penetration of the round. My recommendation would be the Hornady Custom 180gn XTP load.

The foregoing is not intended as an endorsement of anything other than the .38 caliber revolver for self defense; I'm of the considered opinion that, when recoil and terminal effects are considered together, they are still the optimum choice for defensive shooting.

What about +P ammo?

Remember that hollowpoints use part of their energy to expand their diameter, but the energy that's used to expand the bullet is energy that can't used to drive the same bullet forward. There is no such thing as a free lunch; if you want the bullet to expand, it's going to use energy. If there is too little of it to start with, there won't be enough left to carry the bullet on its path.

In those cases the expanded bullet will stop forward movement too soon, which results in very shallow wounds that don't reach vital organs. This is why you don't find a lot of expanding bullets in standard .38 Special cartridges - there just isn't enough energy to drive a bullet deeply into the target and expand it at the same time.

The answer is to start out with more energy, enough to both expand the bullet and penetrate sufficiently. This is often accomplished with "+P" ammunition, which is simply a cartridge which has been loaded beyond what is considered "normal" pressure. The +P loading boosts the energy of the cartridge to accomplish a specific task.

A common misunderstanding of +P loadings is that they're useless since they're not a huge increase in power. Here's the thing: they don't have to be.

The idea behind the +P is to add enough energy to reliably deliver an expanded bullet deep enough to do its job. It doesn't have to be a lot of extra energy - it just has to be enough. If a normal-pressure load can't quite deliver that bullet to where it needs to, but a little hotter +P version does, then that is sufficient for the task at hand.

It's important to understand that you don't need vast increases in power

In .38 Special, the best loads are all of the +P variety.

Federal Nyclad is the only standard pressure round author feels comfortable recommending.

for defensive applications; you simply need enough power to perform both of the tasks we discussed earlier. Some will argue that it's better to have a larger reserve amount of energy on tap than a +P, but everything comes at a price. In the chapters on technique we'll delve into that a little more.

Ammunition for the recoil sensitive

Many people, particularly those with the ultra-light revolvers, find that the recoil of .38 Special +P ammunition is too much to comfortably handle. Sadly, there aren't a lot of alternatives; the Special, in standard-velocity loadings, isn't well known as a fight-ending cartridge.

There is an exception, but unfortunately it's a little hard to find: the Federal Nyclad 125 grain hollowpoint. This load combines a very soft lead bullet with a nylon jacket, which allows it to travel down a barrel without leaving a lot of lead behind. The soft lead expands readily even at .38 Special velocities, but still has a decent amount of penetration. The load has been around for many years and there is a small but reliable number of defensive shootings where it has been used to good (though not spectacular) effect.

It would not be my first choice except for those cases where +P ammunition is contra-indicated.

Chapter 6

REALITIES OF DEFENSE SHOOTING:
THE AMBUSH ATTACK

I remember back when I first entered the defensive shooting world. I'd taken a few classes, read many of the classic books that everyone recommended (and often still recommend, even though they're horribly outdated), and even shot some 'combat' matches now and again (because everyone said that they were a great way to practice "realistically"). I thought I had a good idea of what would happen if I ever needed to use my lawfully-carried gun in self defense.

Then YouTube came along.

The criminal didn't politely stand at twenty-one feet, graciously show his knife, then start running at his victim.

YouTube, along with the other video sharing sites on the internet, started showing dashcam and surveillance camera videos from all over the world.

Hollywood depiction of violence bears little resemblance to the ugly, gritty world of predatory attacks.

What they showed was something of a revelation to me: self defense incidents weren't like what I'd been taught or envisioned. They were fast, violent, nasty affairs wherein the criminal didn't politely stand at twenty-one feet, graciously show his knife, then start running at his victim. Instead he'd wait until he was within just a few feet and then suddenly - and without much, if any, warning - attack.

That was my wake-up call.

BOY, WAS I MISINFORMED!

Even though I consider myself immune to fiction, Hollywood depictions of violence were a lot closer to what I'd imagined would happen than were those gritty videos. But as I watched video after video of people getting severely beaten - or even killed - I slowly learned that the reality of a criminal attack isn't like what we're shown in the movies or on television. What's worse is that they don't even have much resemblance to what many shooting instructors teach. That's because the criminal attack usually happens faster, and with far less warning, than anyone really expects.

Being good at the wrong things isn't being prepared.

After that, I confess I went through several years of being afraid that I wouldn't be able to defend myself with the gun that was on my hip every day. Though I told myself my training was the best available and that my diligent practice reinforced my above average skills (hey, I was even winning local club matches now and again!), somewhere deep in my mind I knew that being good at the wrong things wasn't being prepared.

I recommitted myself to training in ways that were congruent with what I was learning about real criminal attacks. The result is what you're now reading.

EVIDENCE-BASED TRAINING

In the old days of self defense education - a mere thirty or forty years ago - the only basis for training in defensive shooting were the stories that people who had "been there" were willing to tell. Today we know that first-person accounts of traumatic events are rarely accurate[8, 9] but back then we didn't. We took them at face value, and so much of the defensive shooting doctrine from that era is based on participant's flawed, subjective recollections. Much of that doctrine still persists in some quarters.

As time went by, technology and science came to our rescue. Technology in the form of ubiquitous video, like the police cruiser dashcams and video surveillance, made sure that more crimes were caught from an objective viewpoint. The internet played a role as well, because much of that footage ends up online where it can be seen by anyone. Today, any interested student of self defense can do a quick search and find hours of real-life video showing what happens when people are forced to defend themselves. What's scary to the

Ubiquitous security cameras preserve video of actual attacks for later analysis.

uninitiated is that most of those videos show not fights, but attacks - vicious, brutal, targeted attacks. Fights are polite in comparison to the way a predator extracts what he wants from his victim.

At the same time, we've learned a tremendous amount about how the body reacts to a lethal threat. The National Institutes of Health (NIH) says that we've learned more about the brain in the last ten years than we knew in all of recorded history up to that point[10]. This new knowledge includes revelations about how our brain makes decisions in critical situations, how it processes information, and what it directs the rest of the body to do when faced with a lethal threat. Because of this incredible progress in science we now know that there are specific natural reactions to a lethal threat, reactions which can't be trained away or ignored[11].

Any training program on which you embark must be evidence based if you expect that training to hold up in the face of an actual attack. Evidence based training must take into consideration the latest information, both what we know about how attacks happen and what we know about how the body reacts to those threats.

AWARENESS IS A FALLACY

One of the doctrines that came out of the dark ages of training was the idea that some level of generalized 'situational awareness' would keep you safe. There was a time when I too believed that, until I started to see the video evidence. It became clear that there was a serious flaw in that advice, a flaw of which even the least intellectually endowed criminal could take advantage.

The flaw is simple: you can't be completely aware every minute of the day because you have a life to live. No matter how much attention you pay to your surroundings, sooner or later you're going to need to read the menu or watch the movie or supervise your children or look into the eyes of your date. That's life, and those distractions happen hundreds of times a day to even the best of us. (Frankly, if they didn't I'm not sure I'd like my life all that much! Continual paranoia is not fun.)

This isn't to completely discount the value of being aware of your surroundings, only to put it in perspective. You can't be aware of everything around you all the time. You can be aware of some of the stuff all of the time, or all of the stuff some of the time, but not all of the stuff all of the time. At some point you'll return to being human and pay attention to something else. That's just natural.

What's also natural is that this is the point at which you are most vulnerable and, not coincidentally, the point at which the savvy attacker will often choose to initiate contact. Superb situational awareness may only delay the inevitable; an attacker who is sufficiently motivated (i.e., there is something he really wants) to attack a person displaying good awareness may choose to bide

No matter how aware you are, even if you're always swiveling your head, sooner or later something will catch your attention, giving a predator the opening for an attack.

Criminals often set up their own distractions, like asking for the time or directions.

his time, knowing that within a short period of time something will attract the victim's attention - then he can strike.

Criminals often set up their own distractions. While the victim is busy dealing with an innocuous request or conversation ("hey buddy, you got the time?"), the attacker makes his move. Situational awareness can only go so far.

A training regimen which assumes you will always have advance notice of an attack due to superlative situational awareness is fundamentally flawed. It assumes a set of conditions which are probably unlikely to be continually present even with the most conscientious person, and which can be manipulated to facilitate the attack.

AMBUSH: THE PREFERRED METHOD OF THE SAVVY CRIMINAL

Referring back to the work of Tom Givens, we find that the victim was almost always surprised by the attack. I refer to this as the criminal ambush: confronting someone suddenly and unexpectedly in order to commit a crime. Whether the criminal is physically concealed (waiting behind something) or psychologically concealed (obscured by social conditioning or distraction), he strikes when the victim does not know or expect that the attack is coming. The aim is to catch the victim off guard, and it usually works.

It's a little uncomfortable admitting that you can be surprised, but you can be. I can be. I've watched some ardent proponents of the situational awareness defense concept, and I've seen many times in their daily lives when they're distracted enough by things in their normal routine to be surprised. You need to come to grips with the idea that you may be starting 'behind the eight-ball' against your attacker.

This understanding, this realization and admission, is vital. As I noted previously, the ambush is the hardest attack from which to mount an effective defense. If you know ahead of time that you'll be attacked, you can be proactive; you can get into the perfect shooting stance and draw your gun to the perfect sight picture and use perfect trigger control to fire the perfect number of rounds into a perfect group, thus ending the fight. (Or you could just run away before it happens.)

If you don't know the attack is coming until it happens, all of that goes out the window. Your body, conditioned by the inherited survival instincts of the millennia, behaves in a predictable manner that you've probably never before experienced. You don't get your perfect stance or perfect sight picture, and as a result of not training under such conditions, you can't perfectly control your shots like you can on the shooting range. The result is an inefficient response that leaves you exposed to danger longer than is really necessary.

The skills necessary to mount a successful reactive, counter-ambush defense are very different than those used to initiate a proactive defense. As I think you'll see in the coming chapters, what works for the proactive shooting

Think about all the times when you might be surprised - like while taking care of your children's needs, for instance.

doesn't work for the reactive defense. However, the reverse is true - because what works when you're in reactive mode still works when you do have a little preparation time.

Training for the ambush attack allows you to respond to the greatest number of incidents and is therefore the most efficient way to train.

THE COUNTER-AMBUSH TRAINING MODEL

Your defensive shooting training regimen should be based on a counter-ambush training model: reacting to an attack that is surprising, chaotic, and threatening.

It's surprising in the sense that you didn't know it was going to happen, largely because it happened when you were distracted by the normal happenings of everyday life. It's chaotic, in the sense that you don't know what's going to happen next and are forced into reacting to what's happening. It's threatening, in the sense that it poses an immediate and otherwise unavoidable danger to your life or limb - and it's a danger to which the correct response is shooting.

This surprising, chaotic and threatening event is referred to in the Combat Focus® Shooting program as a "dynamic critical incident." That's not a term I use because it's impressive; I use it so that there is no confusion in anyone's mind what I'm talking about. This is a specific kind of attack; it's not a fight, as I've said, because 'fight' implies both consensual violence and a duration that's longer than the typical crime. It's a criminal ambush attack, a predatory attack, that's usually over a few seconds after you recognize that it's happening. It's a very small slice of time, but it's likely to be one of the longest six or eight seconds in your life!

DISTANCE AND THE AMBUSH

As I mentioned in the introduction, these attacks usually happen beyond two arms' reach but - as Tom Given's data shows us - usually within roughly 15 feet. If you think about it, that makes sense; the criminal attacker wants something from you, so he needs to get in fairly close proximity. (This, as opposed to the paid assassin who would simply shoot you from the shadows. Or blow up your car. Or poison your hamburger. You get the idea.)

Since criminals also often use distraction and misdirection to their advantage, they need to get within conversational distance to do so. This tends to explain the data that Givens has collected on those actual attacks his students faced.

The tower sniper or the mall terrorist or the active school shooters are the anomalies, the least likely of threats to face. That doesn't mean that you should completely ignore the possibility of facing one of them, only that you're much more likely to need to deal with the mugger coming around the back of your car and grabbing your door than the deranged killer with a rifle sniping at passers-by. The close-in ambush attack is the most common type of deadly force attack, and is thus the most likely kind of incident you'll have to face. The rest of this book is devoted to helping you prepare for it.

Many attacks happen within conversational distance.

Chapter 7

YOUR BODY'S NATURAL REACTIONS

I f there is any such thing as a certainty in defensive shooting, it's the natural, instinctive reactions that occur when you're surprised by a lethal threat.

Instinctive reactions are those things that humans do without prior exposure or training; they are those things that are seemingly hard-wired in our brains from birth[12]. Reacting to a loud noise, for instance, is a readily observable trait in newborns; babies in the womb, too, are reported to react to a startling sound.

Instinctive reactions to threats have developed over millennia in the human animal; the ability to stay alive among predators, many of them easily able to take down homo sapiens, is why we're at the top of the food chain today. Without some sort of built-in mechanism to automate our responses we likely would not have made it this far.

It's important to understand that these natural reactions happen when you're truly surprised by an attack, and they last for a relatively short amount of time. The half-life of the catecholamine hormones that facilitate your reactions is measured in minutes[13], which means that their effect starts deteriorating very rapidly after the onset of the reactions. Your body's reactions are therefore very short-duration events that, understood and trained for, allow you to gain the upper hand when you're already behind the curve.

One of the salient points regarding your body's natural instinctive reactions is that they can't be trained away. You can learn to suppress their amplitude or to convert them to intuitive responses more efficiently, but they are almost certain to occur. Understanding them is the first step to taking advantage of them.

IDENTIFYING THE NATURAL REACTIONS

When faced with a lethal threat your brain directs your body to make some rather amazing transformations [14]. There are many different reactions, some large and others almost unnoticeable, that enable you to deal with something that poses a threat to your existence. Detailing all of them would be a book in itself.

As it happens, it's not necessary for you to understand all of them. There are only about a half-dozen unique reactions [15] that are important from the standpoint of defensive shooting, important in the sense that they affect how and what you train. In the chapters that follow, you'll find techniques that build on and take advantage of these natural survival reactions, allowing you to respond more efficiently than trying to force an unnatural, artificial technique into the situation (if you even could.)

By training properly you can make the transition from instinctive reaction to intuitive response faster, easier, and without cognitive thought.

EXTERNAL MANIFESTATIONS

Some of the body's natural reactions are external, meaning that they're observable. When you watch surveillance camera footage you'll often see all three of these reactions, all happening approximately simultaneously or, at the very least, in extremely rapid succession. (The order in which I've presented them should not be taken as a timeline of any sort.)

Lowering of the body's center of gravity

If you think about it, preparing for any physical activity - be it running

Lowering center of gravity prepares the body to fight or run, as the situation dictates. Knees bend, body weight drops toward the ground.

away or fighting - requires that the body first drop its center of gravity. Stand in front of a mirror and try to move naturally without changing the height of your belly button; you'll find that you can do nothing more than a robot-like shuffling. When you need to move immediately, like when you're faced with a sudden threat, your body naturally drops its center of gravity to prepare for an extreme exertion. This puts your body in a superb position from which it can lunge or move rapidly to either side, both of which are definite survival positives when facing something that wants to eat you.

This lowering of the center of gravity looks like a shallow crouch; your knees bend causing your body to drop, while at the same time your upper torso leans forward at the hips to maintain balance; the buttocks are forced backward to compensate.

Hands moving toward the line of sight

Humans, as you may have been told, are truly visual creatures. You derive a huge portion of what you know from what you see, and in a lethal encounter that's especially true: what you know of the threat comes mainly from what your eyes tell you. As a result, your mind is hard-wired to protect that most valuable asset.

When people are startled, their hands start to move in a protective manner toward their line of sight; they flinch toward the eyes. They don't always make

When startled, one of the most common reactions is the movement of the hands toward the eyes, to protect the head.

The body's natural defensive position is facing the threat, square on to get best visual information and to make the best use of defensive resources.

it all the way, of course, for a number of reasons (including familiarity with certain stimuli). They do almost always start in that direction, however, and again you can see this very often in videos of actual surprise attacks.

One thing I've noticed is that this flinch, as we'll call it, is convulsive. The muscles that produce the movement tense suddenly and violently, throwing the hands into motion; the shoulders often hunch or roll forward in concert. Sometimes the flinch rises and subsides seemingly without the subject being aware that it even happened.

Orienting to the threat

At the onset of a surprise stimulus the body tends to orient to whatever it is that is identified as being a potential threat. The head turns to put the threat into its line of sight, where binocular vision is at its most useful, and the body usually follows by squaring up to the threat so that it can employ its natural weapons: hands and feet.

This is not a boxing stance, which is a learned position; the natural stance is neutral, in that the body is parallel to the threat and the feet are directly under the body, preparing to move in any direction needed. Any off-axis orientation, such as blading to the threat, would make movement to one side more difficult than the other; it's easy to see how that could be a detriment to survival.

INTERNAL REACTIONS

The external reactions are aided and supplemented by some internal reactions, all of which have to do with changes in blood flow in the body. The blood carries oxygen and the myriad of chemicals which serve to initiate all of the transformations which occur as a result of the threat[16]. As it happens, if you can see the external manifestations we just talked about, you know that these internal reactions have also occurred. The external reactions serve as markers that prove the internal ones are happening as well.

Again, in no particular order:

Increase in resolution in the center of the field of vision

The retina of the eye uses rods and cones to collect and transmit image information to the optic nerve, and that information is sent to the visual cortex where it's interpreted as sight. In the middle of the retina is the fovea, which is populated exclusively by cones, which have higher resolution and faster reaction times than the rods. As a result, the fovea is capable of delivering a much higher level of detail than is the rest of the retina. When the body's alarm response is activated, changes in blood supply to the eye cause most of the information to come from this center where all the cones are located. The result is an increase in resolution, though with a very narrow angle of view. This has a very positive effect on survivability, because it allows the gathering of much more information specifically about the threat.

Reduction in blood flow to the extremities

When faced with a sudden possibility of lethal injury, the body shunts blood from the extremities - hands and feet - to the core. There are several explanations for this phenomenon, but the end result is a decrease in blood to the hands and fingers.

When blood flow is reduced, there is a decrease in strength, dexterity and tactile sensation. Hands might tremble a bit, have trouble doing complex tasks that rely on muscle control, and have less feeling. This sounds entirely negative, but consider the upside: that same reduced blood flow also means that damage to

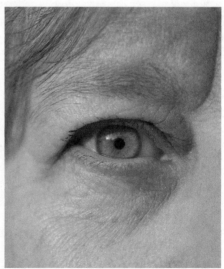

Changes in blood flow to the eye affect focusing and increase resolution in the center of the field of vision.

the extremities won't be felt as keenly, and injuries won't result in dangerous blood loss as quickly.

The downsides of reduced dexterity and tactile sensation are something that we have to work around when we design techniques for handling tools (the gun).

Distortions in the perception of time

One of the more unusual natural reactions is a distortion in the perceived passage of time during a lethal attack. In most cases people report that time slows down, making things appear to be happening at a slower rate - including their own responses to what they're seeing. In reality both the person and the world are still moving at the same speed, but their brains report that they're not.

This becomes a real issue if you have to do anything which requires visual input, since that's where the distortion occurs. Though you may believe you are moving slowly, in reality the rest of the world isn't - which means there is a disconnect between what you think is happening and what actually is.

I've actually experienced this as the result of a severe fright. When I was in college I once parked on a seedy street in a not-terribly-good area of a large city. Walking back to my car I noticed a rather hulking male following me; I quickened my pace, but so did he. I ran to my car and tried to put my key into the door (this was long before the days of remote control locks). I clearly remember trying to get the key in the hole, knowing full well that there was someone closing in, but I couldn't seem to do it fast enough. I tried to speed up but that only caused me to fumble, which in turn fed my panic, which seemed to make things slow down even more! I finally got the key in the lock, jumped into the car and hit the lock button - about the time the fellow ran past me, yelling at a couple of other men on the far end of the block to "wait for me!"

There have been many explanations for why this phenomenon occurs[17] and there is a lot of ongoing research to find out the exact neurological mechanism, but, for our purposes, it's enough to understand that the effect occurs and that it affects both your emotional and physical reactions to what you're seeing.

Interestingly, some people report that time seems to speed up during an incident. Though research is still in its infancy, some of the most important researchers in the field of time distortions suggest[18] that this is a result of training or habituation to a stimulus. Those who have trained certain techniques or maneuvers to the point that they can do them without cognitive thought - without being aware of directing themselves to do those things - usually perceive that they're moving at a faster rate than they really are. This is a very real benefit of training.

In the chapters that follow, I'll be referencing these natural reactions to explain why I make certain recommendations.

WORKING WITH THE BODY'S NATURAL REACTIONS

Why the focus on these reactions? As I said earlier, these reactions affect how and what you train. We go back to our task of efficiency, making the best use of our resources to achieve a specific goal. If the techniques you've trained run counter to what your body actually does when threatened, your response is likely to be delayed (or even circumvented).

A more efficient response happens when you train techniques that work with the body's natural reactions. That's the basis of intuitive skills: things you learn that work well with the way your body works (as opposed to instinctive skills, which are generally considered to be "hard wired" into our brains and require no prior education or exposure).

What is intuitive?

You can learn to do a lot of things that aren't intuitive. Take, for instance, the horn in your car. The horn button is on the face of the steering wheel, usually in the middle or in a place where your open palm can mash it and get sound. In a panic situation your hands are already in proximity because they're on the wheel; all you have to do is flatten your palm and push forward - in the same direction your braking foot is already moving. It also keeps your hand in contact with the wheel, which is a big psychological advantage. Using the horn is a sympathetic movement that requires little to no training, because it works well with what your body is already doing and prefers to do.

Hitting the horn in your car is considered to be an intuitive act because it works well with what your body does naturally.

What if that horn button required you to reach to the side of the steering column and turn a little knob counter-clockwise? You could certainly learn to do it, but when that little kid darts out from between cars, oblivious to your presence, it wouldn't be an easy maneuver to perform. It doesn't work well with anything else your body is doing, and you might not end up doing it at all. It is non-intuitive.

It stands to reason that intuitive skills, those that work well with how the body already functions, are easier to learn, easier to remember and, more importantly, easier to recall when needed because they are a more natural extension of the physical processes that you already do naturally. They are more efficient, and lead to a more efficient response.

Justifying non-intuitive skills?

Instinctive reactions cannot be trained away because they're things that our bodies are hard-wired to do. You can decide to train in ways that work with those reactions or in ways that work against them. In neither case can you replace them.

I've run into many people who insist on training in non-intuitive ways - ways that run counter to what science and medicine (and objective visual evidence) say about how humans react. The justification is usually something like, "I've done it for so long, it's natural to me now."

Things that work against your body's natural reactions are never 'natural.' They may be habitual, familiar from repetition when your instinctive reactions have not been initiated, but that doesn't make them natural. For instance, adopting a bladed boxer's stance because it 'feels natural' works against the body's natural desire to square itself to the target and crouch as it lowers its center of gravity. That special learned stance might be comfortable, but it's not likely to be what happens when your threat responses have been activated.

Habitual? Yes. Familiar? Certainly. Natural? No.

KEY POINTS TO REMEMBER

1) The body's natural reactions are a function of neurology and physiology, and don't vary all that much from person to person.

2) The natural instinctive reactions cannot be trained away, but they can be controlled or converted through training.

3) The external reactions which are visible are markers of the underlying internal reactions.

4) These reactions happen when suddenly confronted with a lethal threat, not so much when you know something is going to happen. Training based on proactive action does not activate these reactions, no matter how 'stressful' it is.

5) Your training needs to take these natural reactions into account if you are to be efficient, because trying to supplant them with non-intuitive techniques is inefficient at best, and more likely impossible in a real incident.

Chapter 8

UNDERSTANDING "EFFICIENT"

To reiterate, this book is about dealing with the threat that you didn't know was coming: the criminal surprise attack - the predatory ambush. If escape is impossible or impractical, your number one concern when you're attacked becomes getting your attacker to stop what he's doing. The sooner that happens, the better for you (and ironically, the better for him, too). The key is to make the best use of your defensive resources to cause the bad guy to go away as soon as possible.

What kinds of defensive resources do you have? Time is certainly a major resource, and the less of it you use relative toward the goal of making him stop the better. Time isn't the only resource, however; ammunition is certainly one, because you only have so many rounds in the gun and/or on your person. Your strength and energy are resources too, and even the space around you can be a resource.

To be efficient in terms of defensive shooting means to make the best use of those resources, or to put it another way, to use as little of them as you can to stop your attacker.

MORE EFFICIENT DOESN'T NECESSARILY MEAN FASTER

It's important to understand the difference between speed and efficiency, and it's common to confuse the two. Doing something faster would certainly seem to be more efficient, and very often in the defensive shooting community the words are in fact used interchangeably.

Speed is an isolated measurement, meaning that it is independent of conditions. Something is faster, something else is slower and the measurement isn't concerned with the reason for the speed to exist, let alone for being measured.

Efficiency, as we'll use it in this book, is using the least amount of the resources at hand in order to achieve your goal.

Efficiency, on the other hand, is dependent on the reason for event; you can't make better use of your resources without knowing what they're being used to do. You're using resources to accomplish something, to reach some sort of goal, and it's only when that something is being accomplished or you're getting closer to the goal that you can determine if you've made the best use of your resources. Efficiency, as we'll use it in this book, is using the least amount of the resources at hand in order to achieve your goal.

Think about this: if you were in your car and your goal was to get to your destination as efficiently as possible, would that mean driving as fast as you could all the time? Of course not; driving faster not only uses more fuel (drag increases with the square of the speed), but it also increases the risk of accidents, traffic tickets and parts breakage. If you wanted to be efficient you'd look at the shortest route, keep your speed as steady as possible, and make a good compromise between travel time and fuel usage.

Efficiency, in other words, is dependent on the context - the circumstances under which something can be fully understood or applied. (You're going to hear more about context in the rest of the book.) Efficiency comes down to making the best use of resources considering the conditions under which they'll be used.

EFFICIENCY IN A DEFENSIVE SHOOTING CONTEXT

The context is what makes evaluating and understanding efficiency in defensive shooting difficult for a lot of people. Let's look at efficiency relative to a task you'll no doubt practice often: reloading your revolver during an attack.

If your only criteria for evaluation of any reload technique were speed, you'd start by using some sort of a timer to measure how long the entire process - or even parts of that process - take. Since the goal of measuring speed is simply to get faster, you'd likely find yourself changing the way you manipulate the revolver, what hand you use to hold the gun and to insert rounds into the cylinder, where you carry your spare ammunition, how you look at the gun to guide your hands, and all sorts of other things large and small to gain even a slight reduction in the time it takes.

Let's take the same task of reloading the revolver and look at it from the standpoint of efficiency: making the best use of your resources under the conditions of their use. You'd first consider what might be happening when you need to do that reload. We talked about the body's natural reactions to a threat stimulus, and here's a good illustration of how they affect what you train: the fastest technique may be less reliable because your natural threat fixation has you watching the bad guy and not your gun; your fine motor skills have degraded, making them shaky and fumble-prone; you're moving, which means your carefully staged positioning becomes impossible; it's dark and you really can't see what you're doing; your ammunition isn't in exactly the same spot you trained with; and so on.

The efficient reload technique takes into account those conditions and the goal itself. The efficient reload technique would reduce (or, preferably, eliminate) the need to look at the reload because it's harder to do so; it would make less use of small muscle groups and fine motor skills, because those skills are degraded; and so on. The efficient reload method is chosen after recognizing and considering all those things that make it more difficult, and working around them to get to the goal more reliably. Reliable things are by nature efficient because they reduce potential hang-ups and bottlenecks.

EFFICIENCY IS DETERMINED BY ENVIRONMENT

Every aspect of your technique is affected by the environment and circumstances of the attack. You can train under some of them, but others (the body's reactions) you can only study and simulate their effect on the technique. Unless you consider both approaches in your training, you'll make the wrong choices - you'll choose speed over efficiency.

Efficiency takes into account the goal: making the bad guy go away with minimum amount of resources at your disposal. Referring back to the reloading example: since the goal has conditions, an efficient reloading procedure takes into account all of the stuff in the environment, stuff that you wouldn't bother with if speed were the only objective.

For defensive purposes, you need to take into account all of the things - including your body's reactions to the threat - that might affect the successful completion of the reload. Once you've identified what is efficient, speed will take care of itself through practice.

Don't try to be faster; focus on being more efficient.

CONSISTENCY IS A BIG PART OF EFFICIENCY

A large part of efficiency is consistency: doing things in the same place and in the same way as much as possible. In the context of the attack, consistency reduces the number of conditional branches - decisions - that your brain has to make to mount a response.

Efficiency applies to the training process, too. You have only so many resources - time, money, energy - to devote to your training. Consistency reduces the number of things that you have to practice, allowing you to make better use of your scarce training resources.

Think of it as recycling - the more times you can repeat specific movements or use specific concepts, the more repetitions you can get into any particular practice session. The more repetitions you get, the more imprints you make in your memory. The more imprints, the easier it is to remember and to recall them.

Consistency isn't the absolute, carved-in-stone, be-all and end-all of efficiency, of course. There may be times (and there's one of them in this book - it comes up in a later chapter) where the most efficient method isn't absolutely consistent with everything else. In that one case I hold to the goal of overall efficiency over sheer consistency. It's a rare exception, however, and consistency is usually a good barometer of what is most efficient. If you're doing something that's inconsistent, or you're asked to believe in something which isn't consistent, there has to be a very cogent explanation of how it is more efficient. Usually there isn't one!

EFFICIENT AND EFFECTIVE AREN'T THE SAME, EITHER

Let's say that you've managed to find yourself in a situation where you really need to shoot an attacker. You panic, draw your gun and start launching rounds in the general direction of the bad guy, firing from the hip or without actually looking at your target. Those rounds go all over, maybe hitting the miscreant - or maybe not, and you don't really know. Are you being effective?

Simply launching uncontrolled rounds at an attacker may or may not be effective - but it certainly isn't efficient!

Of course you are - at some level, anyhow. Even if you don't hit the guy you may cause him to seriously reconsider his chosen profession; he might cower and run away. Even if he doesn't do that, you've certain impacted his ability (and desire) to present a lethal threat to you. Yes, you've been effective - but you certainly haven't been terribly efficient, having used more ammuni-

Purposeful shooting style is both efficient and more effective.

tion, time, and energy than you needed to in order to achieve your goal of making the bad guy stop. Stop he did, but you didn't make particularly good use of your resources to make it happen.

Let's replay that scenario, and instead of panicking this time you quickly draw your gun, sidestep as the gun extends out into your line of vision, drop into a physically strong natural stance and quickly place several accurate shots into his upper chest - at which point he collapses, ending his attack. You've certainly been effective, and judged objectively you've been more effective than in the first scenario. However, the main point is that you've been more efficient: you made the best use of your time, ammunition, and energy to make the bad guy go away faster. Your increased efficiency made you more effective, not the other way around.

Efficient things are effective things, but effective things are not always efficient.

In this book we'll focus on efficiency, because that's the best path to effectiveness. Remember that efficiency only exists in relation to a goal: in this case, stopping the bad guy. If you focus on making the best use of your defensive resources (time, effort, ammunition, space) to make the bad guy go away, you'll be effective. If you only focused on effectiveness, you wouldn't necessarily get your attacker to stop his activities before you ran out of some resource (time, energy, ammunition, or space.)

Things that are efficient are also effective, but not everything which is effective is necessarily efficient!

Things that are efficient are, by definition, effective because you can't achieve a goal without effectiveness. If you focus on efficiency, effectiveness takes care of itself - because if you haven't been effective you can't meet the definition of efficient.

Focus on being efficient. If you truly understand that concept, you'll automatically adopt things that are effective.

Chapter 9

MAKING DECISIONS EFFICIENTLY

When I watch videos of actual surprise attacks, one of the things that stands out is how slowly people respond to the attack. I'm not talking about how slowly they move or shoot, but how slowly they get from the point where the attack starts to the point where their response is initiated. There is usually a gap - some call it a reactionary gap, I call it a time sink - between the points of attack and response. In many cases that gap is the biggest time-waster of the event.

The more efficiently you can make the decision to draw the gun, the sooner you'll be out of danger, regardless of how fast your draw is.

In contrast, I've taken a number of shooting classes, and virtually all of them were focused on things like learning to draw the gun from the holster fractions of a second faster. I've been told that the faster I can get the gun out of the holster, the faster the attack will end. There was a time I believed that, but viewing the objective evidence from many incidents has convinced me that it's not strictly true.

Don't get me wrong - learning to efficiently draw your revolver is certainly important. Having to fumble around or getting the gun snagged in the process will certainly waste valuable time. In this book, though, you'll note that this chapter comes well ahead of the chapter on drawing your revolver. Why? Because the athletic skill of drawing the gun is secondary to efficiently processing information prior to the execution of that skill.

The more efficiently you can make the decision to draw the gun, the sooner you'll be out of danger, regardless of how fast your draw is.

AWARENESS AND PERCEPTION

Believe it or not, there are things going on around you right now that you don't know are happening. More precisely, you're not aware that those things are happening - in the sense of using the cognitive portions of your brain, which afford you the ability to think about what's happening.

You may not know that these things are happening, but your brain does. Confusing? Yes, until you understand that your brain is constantly collecting and analyzing data about everything around you without you knowing it. It perceives - has perception - about what's going on and is making decisions about what to bring up to the level of awareness so that you can actively think about them.

For instance, if you're sitting in your comfortable chair reading this book and a bomb were to go off behind you, your brain would perceive the explo-

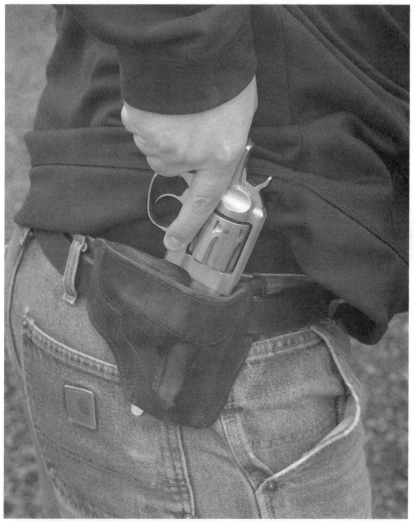

Drawing your revolver smoothly and quickly is certainly important, but so is efficiently determining that you need to!

sion a fraction of a second before you became aware of it. This was brought home to me one day when I was looking at pictures of a mortar attack which happened in Iraq's civil war. There were four people - insurgent fighters - milling around in a building attending to various tasks. There was a photographer shooting pictures of them, and got one frame just as the mortar shell penetrated the wall and detonated. In the picture you can see the fireball just beginning to form at the same instant that a couple of the men are looking at the camera with completely normal facial expressions. Their bodies, however, were already starting to react to the sound and pressure wave of the expanding blast - evidenced by the presence of the external reactions we talked about earlier.

The men weren't yet aware that there was an explosion in the sense that they had cognition or understanding of what was happening, but their bodies had perceived it and had already started to react. It was a chilling picture because, looking at it half a world away, I realized that I knew something that they didn't yet know when the shutter snapped. I knew what was happening before they did. It is so illustrative of the concepts here that I think it's worth bringing up such a disturbing subject.

Your initial startle reactions - your natural reactions - happen because your brain perceives a threat of some sort and that perception initiates your natural survival instincts. It's not until you become aware of the threat that you're able to recognize what's happened and decide how to respond. That awareness happens much more slowly than the perception.

WHERE DOES THE TIME GO? IMPROVISATION IN THE HEAT OF THE MOMENT

Between your body's instinctive reactions that alert you to a threat and the point when you start to draw your revolver are two possible courses of action: one where you improvise a response and the other where you recall and perform a practiced skill[19].

Someone who has never been in a lethal force situation or who has never thought about what he or she would do in response to a deadly attack will be forced to improvise their response. The body's natural reactions serve to alert the analytical functions of the brain - the cognitive processes - which then go to work on a solution. This takes time; while we think of our brains as being very fast, it still takes time for the brain to gather the visual information it needs, analyze what's going on, then figure out the best course of action to take.

If you've trained in techniques that are non-intuitive,
your brain is likely to throw out that training and improvise a
response that will be more in line with its natural reactions.

What kinds of things might the brain have to do? Well, first it has to figure out where the threat is; then it has to deduce what the threat is doing, if it's moving, if the correct response is to use lethal force; then has to direct the muscles to begin the drawstroke, figure out exactly where on the threat to shoot, then actually align the gun on target and stroke the trigger. This doesn't even begin to account for all the other stuff in the middle: Is there an innocent behind the target? Is he holding a hostage? Is he turning and changing the level of precision needed? All of this has to be analyzed and considered in the response. Doing all that takes valuable time.

Interestingly enough, the improvised response is always going to be an intuitive one, because your body is not going to decide to do something that it doesn't do easily - it's not going to choose to do something that doesn't work well with itself.

If you've trained in techniques that are non-intuitive, that don't work well with what your body does naturally, in the compressed time frame of a criminal attack your brain is likely to throw out that training and improvise a response that will be more in line with its natural reactions - a response that is more intuitive.

Evidence, you say? It's on video! This goes a long way to explaining why objective video evidence of a criminal attack almost invariably shows the defender - regardless of prior instruction or experience - adopting a squared-off stance and extending their arms equally in front of them with the gun on their centerline (in and parallel with their line of sight). That improvised response works well with the body's natural reactions of orienting to the target, dropping the center of gravity, and increasing resolution in the center of the field of view. The improvised response is always going to be an intuitive one.

As I said, improvising a response like this takes time - and it's time you can often see in the videos. A classic one I saw shows a police officer stopping a van at night. He nonchalantly walks up to the driver's door when suddenly a large stainless revolver comes out the window pointing right at him. (It's almost like a cartoon; I half expected to see a little "Bang!" flag pop out of the muzzle!) Luckily the criminal's first round is a dud, giving the officer time for his body's natural reactions to start: his center of gravity drops and his hands come up into his line of sight, and the reaction is so complete that his hands try to swat the gun out of the way as a live round discharges.

By this time the officer has moved toward the side of the van and out of the immediate line of fire. He stands there for an instant - almost a full second - before his cognitive mind figures out that he really needs to be shooting at that point. He draws his own gun and returns fire as the bad guy speeds off. The officer's aim is good, and the driver crashes into a power pole perhaps fifty yards away. The attacker will later be pronounced dead at the scene.

That second or so that it took for his conscious thought processes to improvise a response could have cost the officer his life. Could he have done anything to make those thought processes faster, to reduce the time it took for his brain to improvise his response?

The answer is yes, and experts do it every day.

HOW EXPERTS MAKE DECISIONS

There is a growing body of work, such as that of Gerd Gigerenzer[20], which explains how people who are well versed in a subject - experts, we call them - make decisions. As it happens, they've learned to make a connection between things they perceive and their decisions.

Your brain is very good at associating circumstances with outcomes. Even if you're not aware of it, your brain is constantly evaluating the data flowing into it and quickly coming to decisions about what to do. It does this because it's been trained to do it.

Take, for instance, driving a car. Remember when you first started to drive, how much stuff there was to do? You had to keep the vehicle in the lane, moderate the throttle, operate the clutch and gear shift, brake when appropriate (but not so much that you skidded), use the turn signals, spin the wheel just enough to change its direction but not so much that you scraped the curb, and so on.

Now you do all that stuff - and more - without thinking about it; you have become an expert. Over time and given enough exposure to driving, your brain has become accustomed to all the inputs that come from the activity and has automated its responses.

Look at all the controls you use everyday just to get to work - how many of them do you have to think about to use?

The expert responds in an automated way, without having to devote cognitive thought to the process.

Today you can drive down the road and, if a soccer ball rolls out in front of you, you will probably stomp on the brake pedal before you actually think about the ball itself - let alone the child that is likely to be chasing it. That process has become automated; your brain has associated the need to stop the car with the act of hitting the brakes. You don't need to think about picking your foot off the accelerator pedal, moving it over to the brake pedal, and quickly pushing the pedal down with a maximum of force. You respond to an emergency, make decisions about how to deal with it, in an automated way - the way of the expert.

Stomping on the brakes in an emergency isn't something you need to think about; through repetition and experience, it has become an automated response.

In training this is often called a stimulus and response cycle. A stimulus occurs, your brain recognizes the stimulus and then responds to it. This cycle can be within your awareness, as the improvised response is, or within your much faster perception, as is the expert's response.

The expert reacts to a stimulus, recognizes what the correct course of action is, then responds in an automated way based on the course of action, all without having to devote cognitive thought to the process. That's how decisions are made most efficiently.

STIMULUS AND AUTOMATED RESPONSES

To make decisions that efficiently you need to automate your responses. That is, to train in such a way that the choices you need to make occur without you having to think about it.

It's important to emphasize that this process is automated, in the sense that the micro-managing of the response is done below your level of awareness, but not automatic - performed start to finish without your control.

Many people, even some trainers, strive to make shooting an 'instinctive' process. That's wrong on several levels. First, instinctive things are physiological reactions, things that are done as direct consequence of a stimulus and cannot be trained away.

Second, even if we could magically make shooting a truly instinctive reaction, we wouldn't want to. A true instinctive response would have you pulling your gun and shooting your child if she startled you while you were reading the newspaper.

You can, however, automate your responses by training properly. By automate I mean relegating the nuts and bolts of your response to the non-cognitive parts of the brain. Some people rather crudely refer to this as muscle memory, but the expert goes way beyond that.

In Combat Focus® Shooting courses, this is called the Warrior Expert Theory: through frequent and realistic training, experts learn to use the power of recognition to respond to patterns of information more efficiently. Experts make use of the brain's ability to recognize a stimulus, recall the skills necessary, and then respond without needing cognitive thought once the decision to respond has been made.

The decision isn't automated, but the execution of that decision is.

TRAINING FOR AUTOMATED RESPONSES

The goal of becoming an expert is to build the mental links between recognition (understanding that a threat exists) and response (execution of the appropriate skill). The key to doing this, as I just mentioned, is frequent and realistic training.

The frequent part is pretty self explanatory, but it's the realistic part that trips up most people.

The first part of realistic training is choosing to train intuitive skills - those that work well with what your body does naturally. As I hope I've pointed out, non-intuitive skills are not the ones that your body is likely to choose when faced with a truly surprising lethal threat; that's one of the reasons why people often improvise a more intuitive response.

(Non-intuitive skills might work when the threat is anticipated or you're given some space of time in which to prepare. As I pointed out in the chapter on the body's natural reactions, the chemical changes that initiate those reactions are both specific and short-lived. Given time for preparation or time for the chemical changes to wear off, those reactions might be diminished. The available data, however, shows that's not the way that most lethal threats happen. Remember, we're talking about the surprise criminal attack here.)

Since improvisation takes time, and your body is going to do what it does naturally (remember that you can't train away your natural reactions), why not start by adopting techniques that work with what your body is going to anyway? That's both efficient and realistic.

I'll get more into specifics in the coming chapters, but here's an example:

Practicing a non-intuitive stance, one which is not congruent with the body's natural reactions, is not practicing realistically.

practicing a bladed stance with bent elbows is non-intuitive and therefore not realistic. A natural, neutral square-to-the-target stance is what your body wants to do when suddenly faced with a threat, and is realistic.

The second part of realistic training is to practice in conditions that simulate those under which you're likely to need to shoot. This doesn't mean you need fully-furnished shoot house with mannequins; it does mean that you need to practice at unpredictable distances with varying size targets, and with shoot indications that are not known beforehand. We'll explore this in depth in the chapter on practicing realistically.

Ultimately, the goal is that, once you've made the decision to shoot, your intuitive response happens without your having to think about it. You shouldn't need to use your valuable cognitive resources to decide how much deviation control to use or how fast you should shoot or if you need to use your sights or even how precisely you need to shoot. Those things can and should be left to the non-cognitive parts of your brain, the parts that respond more efficiently. That's what the rest of the book can help you do.

Chapter 10

MANAGING SCARCITY

You may not realize it, but you don't have unlimited resources. Even if you are wildly, independently, obscenely wealthy your resources aren't unlimited: you have only so much time and so much energy, and even the biggest bank account can't change the fact that you have only so many hours on this planet.

Why do I mention this? Because the reality that your resources are limited affects your training decisions. You can't really train for everything that could possibly happen to you, because even if you had the money you certainly don't possess the unlimited time on this earth to do so. Your training resources, just like mine and everyone else's, are scarce - and managing that scarcity is critically important to your defensive preparations.

WHAT'S POSSIBLE?

There are all kinds of things that are possible in this world, and I mean 'possible' in the sense that the laws of physics don't preclude them from happening. For instance, as you sit reading this paragraph it's entirely possible that a platoon of North Korean paratroopers could land in your neighborhood and take you and everyone in the vicinity hostage, in exchange for a large shipment of wheat to their country to aid in feeding their starving millions. Again, there is nothing in the laws of physics that would render this impossible - but, let's face it, it's pretty darned unlikely.

If you'd spent all your training time preparing for a North Korean paratroop invasion, however, you'd likely be ill-prepared for dealing with the knife-wielding guy that came around the back of your parked car while you were busy getting groceries from the trunk. Training for the myriad number of things that are merely possible is a waste of your resources because it can leave you with serious gaps in your ability to deal with those things that are

Which is more likely - this scene, or North Korean paratroopers?

far more likely to occur.

If you're going to make the best use of your scarce training resources, you need to first focus on those things that are likely to happen: things that are probable.

PROBABLE BEATS POSSIBLE

Probable things are those events that have some level of mathematical expectation tied to them. In other words, they are things which have happened to others in similar situations frequently enough that it's likely you could face them yourself.

It's these probable events to which you should devote the bulk of your training and practice. I mentioned the work of Tom Givens in the Introduction; his research shows some commonalities which serve to greatly define what is probable. For instance, it's likely that you'll be surprised by the attack, that you'll be between three and five yards from your attacker, that you'll be standing, and that you'll be shooting using both hands with the gun in your line of sight.

Your training time, money, and effort are most efficiently utilized by spending their bulk in responding to an ambush attack (one that you didn't know was coming), within those distances and under those conditions. As I mentioned at the start of this book, those skills will certainly be usable in those cases where you do have some foreknowledge of an attack - but the reverse is not true.

Your probable may not be the same as someone else's. Understanding the crime patterns in your area will help you decide how to bias your training.

What's probable might vary a bit from person to person, because probability is somewhat dependent on the environment. For instance, someone who works on a farm beyond the suburbs faces a different set of daily risks than the urbanite who lives in a trendy housing development. There is some overlap, of course; a home invasion is a home invasion, and the fact that the farmer gets to town frequently and the city dweller goes to the country for recreation every so often means that the bulk of training for each of them is going to be very similar. Still, it's worth spending some time to understand the crime patterns in your area to help you decide how to bias your training. A well-informed instructor should be able to help you with this; if he/she can't or won't, it's probably a good idea to seek better guidance.

Once you've developed the skills necessary to deal with the most probable events, you can expand the conditions under which your skills can be used beyond what is most likely; you can use them to deal with events that are plausible.

PLAUSIBILITY: THE OUTER LIMITS OF TRAINING

If possible things are those that could happen within the laws of physics, and probable things are those that are most likely to occur, plausible things are in between: those with historical precedence or for which there is reason to conclude that they could happen to you.

For instance, the probabilities are that you won't need to shoot with one hand - but it's plausible that you could be injured in one hand and need to shoot with the other, because it occasionally happens. It's plausible that you could need your other hand to hold a flashlight or open a door or protect your child because the way you live your life, the environment in which you live, puts you in those situations with some regularity.

Plausible things might include shooting somewhat beyond the five yards where the best data says attacks usually happen, or the other extreme - in direct contact with your attacker (the techniques for which would fill another book). Some amount of your training, then, should be devoted to those plausibilities.

The Combat Focus® Plausibility Principle says that you should first spend your scarce resources on those things which are likely - probable - and only after that should you expand the range of circumstances under which you can use your skills to embrace the plausible.

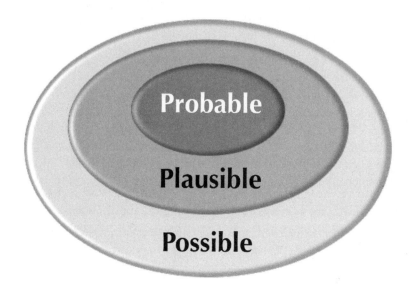

A CAUTION ABOUT PLAUSIBILITIES

Remember that there is often a fine line between plausible (which is a good use of your scarce resources) and what is merely possible (a bad use of your resources.) The problem is that the merely possible is often a whole lot of fun! Running in and out of shoot-houses, negotiating assault towers and shooting 'tangos' on your way down is an adrenaline rush - after all, who doesn't like playing a real-life video game?

You're going to need a hard-nosed attitude with regard to your defensive training resources, because it's all too easy to get caught up in the Walter Mitty fantasyland of shooting instruction. Sadly, a very large portion of the training industry is in fact devoted to things and situations that are distinctly implausible; it's up to you to recognize that and devote your scarce resources to preparing for those things that you may actually face.

What if you succeed in doing that? What if you actually manage (though I doubt it's really possible) to become very well prepared for all of the plausibilities in your life? Wouldn't it be okay to spend some 'me time' playing hostage rescue?

No, I don't think so. Why? Because developing personal safety skills - the reason, hopefully, that you're reading this book - goes beyond shooting, beyond even hand-to-hand skills. If you expand the idea of personal safety, you'll probably discover the need for skills to face a whole lot of very likely life-threatening events that can happen to you and those around you. In fact, the need for these skills is probably more likely than you ever needing to draw your defensive firearm.

What might some of these skills be? It's not often talked about these days, but defensive driving is becoming a more important part of daily life. The road rage incident you have on the way home is probably better handled by learning to drive away from the danger than by practicing shooting out your car window, for instance.

Take severe trauma - the kind that results in massive blood loss. This kind of trauma can be caused by an accident in your workshop, in your kitchen or even while hiking. If you're a bow hunter, you're a slipped step away from a nasty broadhead wound. Knowing how to deal with this kind of trauma, and putting together a kit to help you do so, is probably more important than a weekend playing like you're on a SWAT team.

How's your generator? Your backstock of food? Do you have evacuation kits in your house if you're forced to flee from a devastating fire? Do you have proper extinguishers mounted around your house to help you prevent a little fire from becoming that big one from which you must escape?

If you spend a little time thinking about it, there are more threats to your life than just the bad guy with the switchblade. Spend some of your scarce training resources evaluating ALL of the plausibilities in your life, not just the ones that require shooting.

I realize that as a defensive shooting instructor I'm probably cutting my own throat, but integrity compels me to point out that not every threat to your life is a shooting situation. Make your training decisions accordingly, but remember: your resources are not unlimited. Spend them wisely.

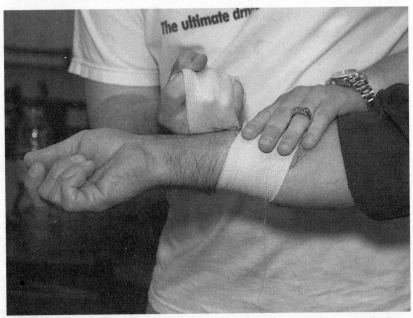

Spending time learning to deal with massive trauma (blood loss) is likely to make you safer than a weekend playing Special Forces soldier.

Chapter 11

FOUNDATIONS
GRASP AND STANCE

Have you wondered why I started this part of the book talking about the body's natural reactions, before even stance and grasp and all the other things most instructors start with? It's because the body's natural, instinctive reactions affect how and what you train - including grasp and stance.

We talked about the external manifestations of your body's reaction to a surprise and lethal threat. One of them was the lowering of your center of gravity; another was orienting to the threat (as well as fixating on it, which is part of the increase in resolution reaction). This is the position you're going to find yourself in automatically when you recognize that you are under a threat.

As I pointed out, these are reactions that you can't train away; they are as close to a certainty as you're going to find in this area of study. The efficient thing to do is to utilize them by structuring your techniques and training around them instead of trying (and failing, for the most part) to fight them.

STANCE

We know that one of the natural reactions is to square off to the target, so start with that. Stand so that your body is parallel to the face of your target, as opposed to being bladed like a boxer. Your feet should be somewhere around shoulder-width apart and roughly on a line with your chest - one foot should not be markedly behind the other.

You'll find that once you're used to shooting in a natural position it's easy to adapt to other, less natural positions if the environment dictates. It's plausible that you could find yourself in a situation where you can't get your feet fully oriented toward the threat at the point you start shooting. That's fine; you can always work around the limitation.

If, however, you do all your training in an exaggerated, staggered-foot or bladed stance and are forced to the other extreme - other foot forward and bladed the opposite direction - you'll find it much harder to efficiently re-

Natural, intuitive stance puts shooter square to target, feet apart, lowered center of gravity.

Lowered center of gravity is much like a shallow crouch.

spond. Starting at a middle ground, so to speak, makes it easier to go to either extreme than it is to spend all your time at one extreme and then try to go to the other when threatened.

Before your body can move or mount a defense it's necessary to lower your center of gravity. This natural reaction can be duplicated in training by bending your knees and throwing your buttocks backwards six to eight inches. This also forces your upper body forward, and I tell my students to think of it as a shallow crouch because that's what it most closely resembles. This is the fighting/movement position that humans adopt naturally when surprised. It's maneuverable and resistant to forces like punching and shoving. Coincidentally, it's also superb for resisting the recoil forces of a revolver!

With your torso and feet oriented to the threat and your center of gravity lowered, you're in an absolutely textbook position of natural reaction. It's from this natural, neutral position that we'll add the tool - the revolver - that we'll use to end the confrontation.

GRASP AND READY POSITION

If you'll re-read the chapter on trigger control you'll find the step-by-step instructions for the correct grasp. Remember that your training is going to be geared to delivering rapid, multiple, combat-accurate hits on target; if your grasp is weak or intentionally light like a target shooting technique, it is going to make that task very difficult. Proper grasp within your limits of strength

Start with the high compressed ready, from which you'll be able to do a number of things. Consistency!

is the key to controlling your revolver's recoil, and the smaller and/or lighter your gun the more important it becomes.

Once you've achieved a good grasp on the revolver, bring it into what Combat Focus® Shooting refers to as the high compressed ready (HCR). The revolver should be close into your body, with your elbows tucked into your sides. The barrel should be pointing roughly at the target, or perhaps just a little lower, but never higher. The revolver should be somewhere around the base of your sternum, but no lower than your navel.

This is a consistent position from which a number of techniques will originate. Remember what I said about consistency being a big part of efficiency? This is one of those instances where it shows itself - as you'll see, getting used to presenting the gun from this spot will pay dividends.

EXTENSION

From the high compressed ready and while in that natural, neutral stance, simply extend the gun forward, into and parallel with your line of sight. Your arms should extend an equal amount, as opposed to one of the artificial, non-intuitive positions where one is bent and one isn't, or one is bent one way and one is bent another. (I'll have more to say about this in the next chapter.)

Simply extend your arms equally to bring the revolver into and parallel with your line of sight.

The last 1/4 to 1/3 of the extension should be straight out to the target.

The gun should be into your line of sight before you finish your extension. The last 1/4 to 1/3 of the extension should be straight out to the target.

It's important that the gun come into your line of sight and finish extension while parallel to it. A large part of getting proper index on target, and settling the gun prior to firing the shot, is making sure that that gun is not moving up or down relative to the target just before shooting. If you were to come up from the high compressed ready directly to the shooting position, the gun would still be moving upward as you reach full extension. You would then need to stop that upward movement and bring the gun back on target before you could shoot.

By bringing the gun immediately into your line of sight - at no more than roughly 2/3 of full extension - and finishing the extension by traveling parallel to your line of sight directly toward the target, you eliminate the need for a time-consuming elevation correction. It's a more efficient way of achieving a fast and sure index on the target.

THE VIDEO REALITY

When I look at objective evidence of brutal attacks, such as dashcam or surveillance videos, I consistently see - regardless of the level of training - that people adopt a shooting stance very much like I've outlined here.

The body's natural reactions dictate the physical positioning: lowered center of gravity, squared off to the threat, forward weight bias. Why the equally extended arms? That has a lot to do, I believe, with the way our visual systems have evolved to use tools (more about that in the next chapter).

My point is that what I don't see - and have never seen - is the exaggerated Weaver or Chapman-type stances that were once so common in defensive shooting instruction. As you've learned, the human body does very specific things when confronted with a lethal threat, and the available evidence supports the scientific contention that training doesn't really affect those things all that much.

If you know ahead of time that these are the things you are likely to do when surprised by a threat, doesn't it make sense to train and practice them? That's what intuitive skills are: skills that work well with what your body is going to do naturally. Doing anything else is non-intuitive and ultimately inefficient, both in terms of your training time and your responses to a threat.

Chapter 12

WHAT IS PRECISION IN DEFENSIVE SHOOTING?

Y ou're looking at two targets, let's say of the IDPA variety where there is an eight-inch central circle representing the optimum defensive shooting area (what is usually called the 'A-zone'). On one target there are a half-dozen shots scattered inside the circle, while on the other those same half-dozen are in a tight little group in the middle of that circle. Which shows a better understanding of precision from the standpoint of a defensive shooting?

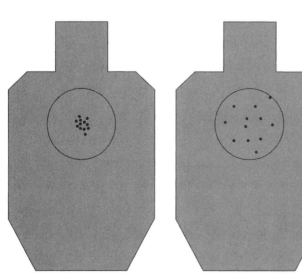

Which of these targets shows a better understanding of precision in defensive shooting?

Before you answer, remember that the goal in defensive shooting is to make your attacker stop - using the least amount of your resources as possible. In other words, efficiently. Is taking the time and energy to achieve smaller groups really a mark of good, efficient defensive shooting?

I'd say no. It certainly is a display of athletic shooting prowess, but it's not efficient because of the time and energy it takes to achieve that level of precision when it isn't needed.

WHAT IS PRECISION?

Many people use the terms accuracy and precision interchangeably, but they're not the same. In defensive shooting they represent two very different concepts, and it's important to understand those.

Precision, as we'll use it, refers to the area in which you need to place your bullets. In our IDPA target example, the precision needed is represented by the A-zone circle. Every shot within that circle is worth exactly the same amount as every other shot.

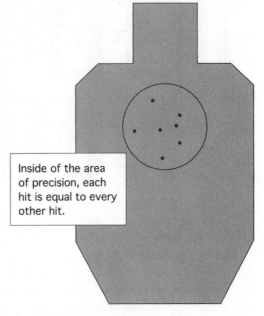

Inside of the area of precision, each hit is equal to every other hit.

In defensive shooting, the area of precision is similar in concept: it's that area in which each shot will contribute the maximum amount to stopping the attack. (We know, of course, that there are huge variables in the effect of any particular bullet, and the effect can vary with fractions of an inch of placement, but we also know that targeting vulnerable areas - such as the high center chest - will lead to the most rapid incapacitation by doing the maximum damage to vital functions.)

If you take nothing else from this discussion, take this: the target determines the precision needed, not the shooter.

The target, which in the case of defensive shooting is your attacker, determines the precision needed by what is exposed. For instance, the bad guy could be crouching behind a car with only his head and shoulders showing. In that case, the area of precision is very different than if he were standing directly in front of you. The dictated area of precision varies, and the target is in charge. It's your job to recognize what that area is and recall the skills necessary to deliver that level of precision.

If your attacker - your target - changes position or alignment, the area of precision changes as well.

WHAT, THEN, IS ACCURACY?

Accuracy, on the other hand, is a measure of whether or not any given bullet you fire actually hits within the area of precision that you've recognized. If your shot hits within that area, it is accurate. If it doesn't, then it is not accurate. Accuracy is a digital concept; it is yes or no. Either you delivered the precision needed, or you did not.

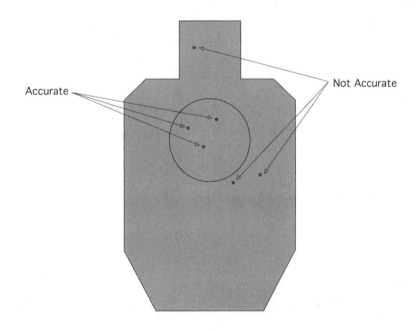

Accurate

Not Accurate

Think of a shooting match where you're using the ubiquitous eight-inch steel plate. Any hit on that plate will flip it over, but any miss will leave it standing there to mock you. (I speak from experience!) If you hit that plate, it doesn't matter where you hit it; a hit is a hit is a hit. If the bullet connects with the steel, the plate will go down and you get the credit.

If you deliver the amount of precision dictated by the target, you win. If you didn't, you lose. Accuracy is whether you hit the target as it has been defined by itself.

YOU CAN'T BE "MORE ACCURATE"

Because accuracy is a state of achieving the required level of precision, there is no such thing as "more accurate" or "less accurate"; either you hit where you intended/needed to, or you didn't. This is a hard concept for many people to understand, because the standard for many years has been to learn to shoot more and more precisely: into smaller and smaller areas. Once you realize that you don't get to choose the area of precision you'll understand that your job is to simply place your bullets into the area that the target has determined. The measurement of your success is whether you were able to. Precision is best thought of as accuracy inside of a specified area.

Can you choose to shoot to a greater level of precision? Yes, you certainly can - at least, on the training range. The problem is that it doesn't make any sense to do more than the target requires because you have to give up something else to do it.

For instance, you could certainly choose to shoot each of those steel plates dead center rather than accepting a hit anywhere on their surface. The results - the toppling of the plate - are identical in each case. Since your job is to recognize the level of precision that the target requires, choosing to shoot to a greater level of precision than what is needed does nothing for your ability to

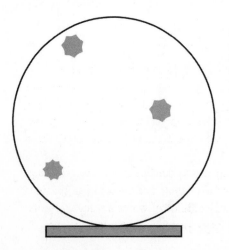

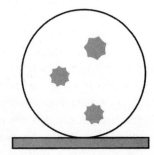

Shooting to a greater level of precision than needed isn't practicing realistically; shooting to a greater level of precision because the target demands it is.

understand the target.

If you want to shoot to greater levels of precision, it's better to use targets which demand a greater level of precision. Then you get the practice not just of delivering the accuracy needed, but also recognizing the precision required. The two go together.

THE REALITY OF STOPPING THE THREAT

If you are to stop your attacker, you have to accept that you're going to need to damage his vital organs and functions. You need to do the right kind of damage, and you need to do enough of it.

It's possible to cause the right kind of damage, but not enough of it; it's also possible to cause a lot of damage, but not of the right kind. You have to do both!

Is it likely that a single shot will do enough damage to cause your attacker to stop? No, it's not.

Is it likely that a single shot will do enough instantaneous damage to cause your attacker to stop? No, it's not. There are certainly those rare occasions where a single shot might do that, but that's not something your can depend on. You must acknowledge that stopping a threat will most likely require a quantity of damage that can only be obtained with multiple shots. Those shots will do the best job of doing so when they land within the area of precision that the target has dictated.

In a defensive shooting incident the target predetermines the precision necessary, not actively, but simply because of its physiology, its construction - where the important bits are located. Human physiology is pretty static, but the precision needed to affect it changes because the target (and you) operate in three-dimensional space. The shape of the physiological target changes with angle, height, position and posture.

ACCURACY IS EFFICIENT!

Let's say that in a particular incident the precision needed, the area of maximum damage by any given bullet, encompasses an area the size of your hand. To be accurate, your shots would have to land inside of that area. (Don't misunderstand: the damage that inaccurate shots do may in fact be valuable and disruptive, but that damage isn't equal to that caused by the shots which land in the target area itself.)

Since your job is to do rapid and significant damage inside that area, and inaccurate shots don't do as much of it as accurate ones, they waste the time, energy and ammunition that you expended. In other words, inaccurate shots are inefficient. Remember that inefficiency simply gives the bad guy more time to hurt you or the people you're protecting.

Here's the important thing: once you've achieved the necessary accuracy, any attempt to shoot more precisely than that needed by the target is wasteful too. If you accept the idea that shots landing inside of the area of precision dictated by the target are doing the maximum damage already, and that each hit is going to be roughly equal to every other hit, then trying to place shots closer together (shooting to an artificially inflated level of precision) doesn't do you any good. It does, however, waste time. What is a wasted resource? Inefficient!

This is why I pointed out that you should be focusing on efficiency rather than effectiveness. Things that are efficient are by definition effective, but effective things are not necessarily efficient. Delivering an artificially inflated level of precision, that beyond which the target demands, requires additional time and effort which may not be justified by meaningful effect on the attacker. This extra time and effort for any given shot is wasted, and could be better used in delivering another shot (doing more damage). The expenditure is inefficient.

If you're already hitting all shots in the heart, for example, attempting to concentrate those shots in the left ventricle doesn't really achieve anything additional. You're already doing the maximum damage, and the extra time and effort that it takes to achieve this unneeded level of precision could be better spent shooting more and doing more damage.

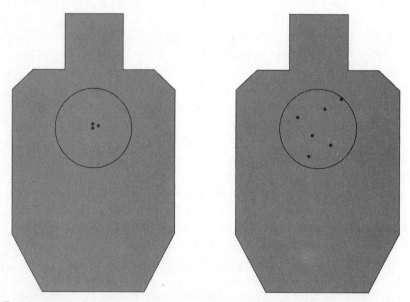

To make your attacker stop, you need to do more damage. Shooting additional accurately placed rounds does that more efficiently than shooting fewer shots to an arbitrarily greater level of precision.

Once the precision threshold has been reached it's the number of shots, not how close to each other they land, that will determine the damage that stops the threat. The more rounds that hit, the faster your threat is going to stop.

Making your shots accurate, meaning that they are all landing in the area of precision dictated by your target, is the most efficient way to stop the threat. Since everything in defensive shooting is (or should be) evaluated by its effect on the target, and higher levels of precision beyond the threshold required do not result in greater effect, attempting to be more precise is a waste of time and effort.

You either are, or are not, accurate; there is no such thing as 'better' once the threshold has been crossed. Not being sufficiently accurate is inefficient, and attempting to deliver a greater level of precision than the target dictates is inefficient as well.

RECOGNIZING THE PRECISION NEEDED

In a previous chapter I talked about what it means to be an expert, in this case about defensive shooting. Through frequent and realistic training, you can use your brain's ability for recognition to make more efficient decisions. This is true for the precision that the target dictates.

If you are attacked, you'll have a lot of decisions to make in a very short period of time. One of them comes after the could-should decision (the one where you decide that lethal force is necessary): exactly what it is that you're going to shoot.

You already have a little foreknowledge about the level of precision that might be necessary, simply because you know

Which target will you be asked to shoot next? There are several levels of precision needed on this target, and it's only when the command is given that you will know - recognize - what level of precision the target is demanding. That's realistic practice!

a little about anatomy. You'll have to wait to find out exactly what precision the target dictates, because you don't know what part of himself the attacker will present to you. Precision may be dictated by the target, but is it has to be recognized by you - the shooter. Your target is in control of the circumstances, but you are in control of your response to those circumstances.

If you train with random-sized targets, called randomly by a partner, you will start to develop that recognition and recall sequence necessary for expert-level response. If you don't know which target is coming next, you won't know ahead of time the level of precision it dictates. Training in this manner allows you to get the experience in quickly determining the level of precision, and then recalling the skills (control over the gun) which allow you to place accurate shots.

This kind of randomized practice helps you to learn to recognize what must be shot, recognize the precision that it dictates, and then recall the physical skill of deviation control to get your hits. This process is far faster than cognitive thought, and is much better suited to adapting to the rapidly changing environment of a fight.

I'll go into this in more detail in the chapter on practicing realistically.

RAPID, MULTIPLE SHOTS

As I've already mentioned, it is unlikely that a single shot is going to take your attacker out of commission. Multiple shots, delivered quickly, do that job.

As it happens, delivering the necessary accuracy for the first shot and for each additional shot requires the same physical skills: command over the gun that reduces the area in which the bullets might land. That concept is called deviation control, which I'll talk about in detail in the next chapter, but for now it's enough to point out that in order to hit a smaller target, or one further away, you need to apply more control over the gun. If you're going to fire more than one shot - and you likely will need to do so - you'll have to apply that deviation control continuously and dynamically.

The difference is in continuity; if you know you're only going to fire one shot, you'll tend not to apply the necessary post-discharge control that sets you up for the next shot. If, on the other hand, you accept the possibility that you'll be firing more than one round, you will automatically apply the appropriate follow-through that keeps you on target. To deliver the level of precision needed by the target for the first and each additional shot, the basics - stance, grasp, trigger control, and all the rest - need to be consistent and continuous.

EXPANDING YOUR UNDERSTANDING OF PRECISION

When you consider that defensive shootings are dynamic and chaotic events, it becomes obvious that levels of precision cannot be exactly defined.

Going back to the discussion about aiming for the heart, though it may be the very best route to target incapacitation, it's probably not going to be practical to aim for it specifically while everyone (you and your attacker) is in motion - the likely state of a violent attack.

This is why precision from the standpoint of defensive shooting is impossible to define exactly. If an instructor folds a piece of paper in half and says "that's a good defensive group," he's predefining something that may or may not have any basis in reality.

The level of precision that you recognize has to be that where any given bullet can be expected to contribute the maximum amount to stopping the attack. If your attacker is facing you directly, squared off to you, that area is probably going to be his high (upper) center chest. Shots in that area are likely to do significant damage to his ability to present a threat to you, and over time have come to be accepted as the most reliable way to disable an opponent over a wide range of circumstances.

Note that I didn't say something like "an eight-inch circle in the upper chest area." The exact size of that area is determined by the physiology of the attacker - bigger people are likely to have bigger chest cavities, while with little runts like me that circle covers the shoulders. Applying the bigger guy's level of precision to me means that a lot of bullets will not be hitting in tremendously vital areas!

ARE ALL HITS REALLY EQUAL?

From a purely intellectual standpoint, we know that a shot that actually hits the heart is probably more valuable than one that simply hits a lung. However, it's not efficient to try to place shots at that level of precision with a handgun during the kind of chaotic, threatening incident we're talking about. It's entirely possible that both you and your attacker will be moving - either trying to attack (him) or keep from being attacked (you.)

Instead, you settle for a level of precision that will do the job of stopping your attacker while at the same time actually being achievable in the chaos of the attack. This level of precision has to accommodate not just the physiology of the attacker, but the reality of the environment and of the circumstances under which you're shooting.

This is why it's important to understand that precision is recognized. The exact circumstances of your attack will all contribute to your recognition: how he's standing relative to you, if there are intermediate barriers that will absorb or deflect your bullet, the assailant's size and more all play a part in determining the precision dictated by the target - and they might change during the course of your defense.

The most vital part that can be reliably hit is the level of precision necessary.

If the attacker turns slightly to one side, then your recognition changes as

What's the precision this target is dictating?

his vital area narrows slightly. If he ducks behind a trashcan, the area of precision changes again.

As I've already pointed out, trying to achieve a greater level of precision than required in any specific situation is inefficient (using more time and effort), and may not even be possible given the short time frames of the typical attack.

WILL BECOMING A 'BETTER' SHOOTER HELP?

Seeking artificially high levels of precision, beyond what the target requires, during an incident is counterproductive to efficient defensive shooting. Working to simply become a better shooter, in other words spending time learning to deliver artificially high levels of precision, may not be the best way to train to survive violent encounters.

As we've seen, there isn't a single level of precision appropriate to all encounters. Your need for accuracy (actually hitting the target area) doesn't change, but the recognized precision (which tells you how carefully you need to shoot) certainly does.

Efficient training focuses on delivering appropriate levels of precision, on demand and without cognitive thought.

Your highest efficiency in training is attained by focusing your efforts on being able to deliver appropriate levels of precision - no more, no less - on demand and without cognitive thought. The recognition of the precision needed should trigger a recall of the skills necessary to achieve it.

Shooting the same target over and over, focusing only on speed, is not practicing realistically. You have nothing to recognize (or, more precisely, nothing to practice recognizing) because the precision needed has been statically and arbitrarily predetermined. Your drills become a choreographed and overly mechanical test of muscle control, and you end up focusing on anticipation of the shot as opposed to recognition of the need to shoot.

In order to build the recognition and associative recall ability that makes for expertise, you must reduce anticipation by including options in your drills. Those options must be presented randomly, forcing you to recognize the precision needed and then recall the necessary skills to make accurate shots inside of that area.

It's the association of the recognition and the recalled skill that forms the links necessary for highly efficient decision-making to happen. That can't occur unless, for any given drill, there is more than one option and it's presented randomly.

Any attempt to define a 'good defensive shooting group,' regardless of what the definition may be, dooms the process to failure because there is no opportunity to practice recognition.

Chapter 13

BALANCE OF
SPEED AND PRECISION

No matter how long you've been shooting, you've probably realized that to achieve greater precision - accuracy inside of a smaller area - you need to take more time. You also probably realize that if you shoot faster, taking less time, you'll give up some precision. That's the tradeoff in defensive shooting, and every situation has a different balance of speed and precision.

All defensive shooting (all shooting, really) is a balance of speed and precision, and always has been. I have hunting books written in the early 1960s where the author talks about this concept, so it's not exactly new. Thinking about it and systematizing it is new, however, and I believe that the Combat Focus® Shooting program was the first to approach it in a very analytical manner. The Balance of Speed and Precision has become one of the core concepts in that program because it is so important to becoming a more efficient defensive shooter.

WHAT IS YOUR BALANCE?

The optimum balance of speed and precision for any situation will be determined by a combination of you, your attacker and your environment. Change one factor, and your balance of speed and precision - you at your most efficient - will change as well.

Even in an identical scenario, two different shooters will have different balances because they have different capabilities and levels of competency. Even your own balance will change from day to day (or even hour to hour) as your level of fatigue changes.

Inside of your environment there are a wide number of variables that affect your balance, and realistic training helps you to experience and understand those variables. The size of the target, your distance from the target, the conditions under which you shoot, and even your anticipation of the need to shoot all affect your balance of speed and precision.

The target dictates precision

The target, as we've already discussed at length in the previous chapter, dictates the precision needed. If it's a paper target, the scoring or hit zones are predetermined; for an attacker, his physiology and his position relative to you dictate the precision you need to deliver.

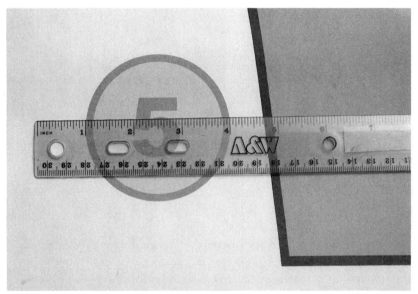

The target determines the precision needed; you can't change it, you can only recognize it.

Your job is to recognize the precision that the target dictates, but remember that you can't change it. You could decide to shoot to a greater level of precision, but I hope you now understand that it's inefficient (or even functionally impossible) for you to do so.

Your skill determines your hits

Your skill - or, more precisely, your application of your skill - determines whether you land the shots you need. In other words, your skill determines your accuracy.

No matter how good a shooter you are, there is always some variability between where you intended the shot to go and where it actually lands. Some people have more deviation between aim and hit than others, but everyone's shots will deviate some. Controlling the amount of deviation will mean the difference between an accurate shot, one which hits within the target area, and one which doesn't.

Deviation control is the mechanism by which you exercise your application of skill, and it takes both time and effort. The amount of deviation control you need also varies; a large target area in close demands less deviation control than a smaller target area which is further away. In cases where the precision needed is rather loose you can get away with less deviation control, which means that you can shoot faster.

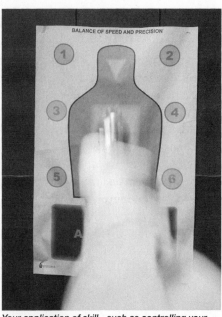

Your application of skill - such as controlling your muzzle deviation - determines whether you get the hits you need.

As more precision is needed you'll be forced to apply more deviation control - more skill - if you are to land accurate shots. That is going to take more time.

What causes deviation? You might not have good alignment on the target. This can be due to using the alignment guides (sights) incorrectly or simply not having the gun in and parallel with your line of sight if not using them. You may not have mastered the trigger stroke, and instead of staying steady the muzzle moves off target as the trigger is compressed - or off target when the hand relaxes as the trigger is released. Some people blink just before the shot goes off, disrupting the visual contribution to alignment. A loose grasp can contribute to excessive deviation, and if you're not solidly planted - feet not moving - when the shot breaks, or if you're still in the process of extending, your deviation will increase.

To reduce deviation, you must apply your skills. A proper sight picture (where appropriate), better trigger control, a strong unwavering grasp, and making sure that you have a solid stance before you stroke the trigger are some of the ways to do that. On the practice range, this takes some concentration. The point of practicing is to develop the ability to apply the skills without having to think about it.

Your confidence determines your speed

It might seem odd that your confidence is in control of your speed, but it is. Confidence in your own abilities determines how fast you'll shoot (unless you're shooting out of panic).

I'm not referring to confidence in terms of your personality or emotional makeup; instead I refer to the correlation between what you think you can do and what you really can, which is a product of your training and practice.

Lots of people train under a specific set of circumstances constantly, never varying what they do to any significant degree - same targets, same distance, same stance, same everything - except trying to do it faster each time. This is the basis, in fact, for standards and benchmarks: an unvarying set of conditions under which objective measurements can be made.

This idea comes to us from the competition side of shooting, where sports medicine meets scoring rings. It is based on the belief that shooting is a purely physical or athletic activity that needs to be quantified. This works only as long as you can control the variables; since you can't control the variables of an attack, this approach leads to an unrealistic understanding of your own limitations.

Let's say that you train using a fixed course of fire. Since you've done it many times, you know that you can draw and fire two rounds on target in, say, 1.5 seconds. Remember: that's when you know you're going to shoot, you know the distance, you're in a perfect stance, you know what your target is and where it is, and you've rehearsed the entire sequence in your mind.

Now do the same thing - only you're at the bus stop holding your child's hand and looking expectantly down the road when someone comes up behind you with a knife. You now have to process the threat through your mind, orient to the threat, fire more than two rounds, and instead of that nice Ruger GP100 range gun on your hip you've got one of the ultra-light Smith & Wesson Centennials loaded with hard-kicking +P rounds in your pocket.

What's likely to happen? Your over-confidence and lack of realistic practice probably results in trying to draw and shoot at the same rate you do your phenomenal double-taps on the calm shooting range. Ever shoot a lightweight revolver too quickly? Then you know what happens to your deviation control: it usually gets very poor.

Understanding your actual ability will keep you from being under- or over-confident.

You'll attempt to shoot too fast because you've not trained under conditions that you just experienced. The result is greater deviation (less accuracy), which, as we've already discussed, translates to being inefficient.

Being under-confident also stems from not training realistically - for instance, always using your sights in practice because you 'can' rather than you 'need to.' When the attack happens, you of course default to attempting to employ them, despite not really being able to (body reactions) or really needing to (target very close.) Between doubting your ability to shoot using the threat

Shooting the same choreographed drill under controlled conditions does not increase your confidence to recall skills on demand!

focus you're forced into, and taking time trying to line up your sights just like you do on the range, you might end up shooting more tentatively. Again, the response is inefficient: wasted time.

The way to correlate your skills and your confidence in those skills is to train under the expected (probable) shooting conditions. That means practicing with random targets and distances, under different conditions, to develop a mental spreadsheet of what you can/need to do under many combinations of factors. Understanding your actual ability will keep you from being under- or over-confident, shooting too slowly or too quickly. You should always be shooting as fast as you believe you can get the hits, and realistic practice is how you come to a fact-based belief under any given set of variables.

FACTORS THAT AFFECT YOUR BALANCE

I mentioned above that there were a number of things which directly affect your balance of speed and precision. First, of course, is the size of the target: that area which you recognize as being the optimum for rapid and reliable incapacitation in your attacker, or that which is delineated for you on the practice range target.

Not understanding the factors that affect your balance of speed and precision, and, moreover, not training under as many variations of them as possible, will give you an incomplete picture of your own abilities. It's that incomplete picture that causes people to shoot at a rate other than what their ability allows, producing an inefficient response.

Size of the target

It's deceptively simple: the smaller the target area, the more deviation control you must apply to get your hits. The more control you need to exert, the more time and effort it's going to take. The larger the target area, the less deviation control you'll need to get accurate hits, and the faster you'll be able to shoot.

Delivering higher levels of precision takes time and effort and illustrates the need to train to what the target requires, rather than to some arbitrary standard. It goes right back to the confidence issue; shooting at artificially higher levels of precision than needed leads to a lack of correlation between what you can do and what you believe you can do.

Distance to the target

In handgun training it's fashionable to ignore distance to the target and instead focus on the size of the target. The rationale behind this is that as you get further away the target appears smaller, and therefore paying attention to the size automatically takes care of the distance as well.

That's not entirely true, for a couple of reasons. First is the psychological effect of distance; I've observed that if there is a small target at a very close distance, most students will think that's pretty easy to hit. Whether that's the case in reality isn't important, because the student believes it is and usually delivers the hit. There's a very real value to the belief in one's abilities, as the discussion about speed pointed out.

Take a larger target further away, so it appears to be the same size as a small target up close, and I've found most students start to choke. There seems to be a fear about shooting at extended distance, as though it's some esoteric skill that only 'advanced' shooters are able to master. It's not true, of course, but as distance increases so does the student's anxiety level.

It doesn't take a lot of distance for that to happen, either. I've noticed that simply doubling the distance from, say, ten to twenty feet is enough to trigger some degree of performance anxiety in most students. (That's getting to be at the outside of the most likely engagement distance, but still well within plausibility based on Tom Givens' data.)

One of the interesting phenomena relating to the psychological effect of distance is that more experienced shooters tend to start compensating for an imagined bullet drop. (For those who are new to ballistics, the pull of gravity combined with air resistance causes bullets to drop in a smooth and predictable arc as they travel.) This is a concern with rifles at extended distances, but with handguns it usually doesn't start to make a difference in the point of impact until it gets out in the fifty yard range (a typical defensive load will hardly drop at all at twenty-five yards). Intentionally "holding high" happens to a lot of shooters even when the distances are well under twenty-five yards, and often leads to rather substantial difference from where they thought the bullets would land.

Distance to the target, regardless of size, makes a huge difference - much of it psychological - on the balance of speed and precision.

The other major issue with target distance is that deviation increases as the range increases. Any amount of muzzle movement from the point of aim is magnified by distance, and the control necessary at ten feet is insufficient at twenty. At close distances, reducing the target size requires an obvious increase in deviation control, but at extended distances the amount of control required is more than the apparent size of the target might indicate. Only training at these varying distances, ideally to the outside edge of plausibility, will acquaint the shooter with the issues involved.

I've found that an occasional - and I do mean occasional - drill shooting at unreasonable distances (say, in the 25- to 50-yard range) will help cement these concepts in a student's mind. This should only be done after achieving competency at the plausible shooting distances, however.

The conditions under which you shoot

You, your attacker and the environment in which the attack happens all dictate the conditions under which you'll shoot. The light level, temperature, whether it's raining, your level of fatigue, your familiarity with your gun, the surface on which you're standing, people around you - all of these will affect your balance of speed and precision.

Most of those should be self explanatory, as they affect you physically. Can you see your attacker clearly? Can you handle your revolver easily? Can you get a good grasp on the gun? Is it so cold you're shivering? So hot you're sweating? All of these, and more, will have an effect on you your balance of speed and precision.

Your familiarity with your revolver will impact this balance as well. If you're used to shooting a customized Smith & Wesson but need to use a Ruger SP101 in self defense - having not shot it all that much - the difference in size, trigger operation (feel, weight and length of travel), sights, grips, and the location of the cylinder release button will all affect how you shoot. It's worse if you spend most of your shooting time practicing, training and competing with an autoloader but carry a five-shot revolver most of your waking hours.

The perceived penalty for a miss

Imagine this scenario: you're walking through a park and round a corner toward the playground only to encounter a man threatening you with a knife. You smoothly draw your gun as you move laterally off the line of attack, and fire sufficient shots to cause your attacker to collapse. Good job!

Now, think about two different variations: same park, same attacker, same time of day, same weather, same playground, same everything - except in Variation 1, the playground is empty; in Variation 2, the playground is filled with children.

Is your balance of speed and precision going to change between those two scenarios? Are you going to shoot slower in one than the other?

Imagine this fellow attacking you, but the playground filled with children. Think that might influence how you shoot?

For most people, the answer is yes. Shooting at an attacker against the backdrop of a full playground brings home the consequences of not delivering accurate shots to the target area: a miss might hit an innocent bystander. I'm not suggesting that you train for this by shooting around live targets - there are some trainers who do, and I consider it highly reckless - but understand that just because you can really whip those shots out when there's no penalty doesn't mean you can do so when something important is on the line. Your perception of the penalty for missing will affect how you shoot (and sometimes whether you shoot at all.)

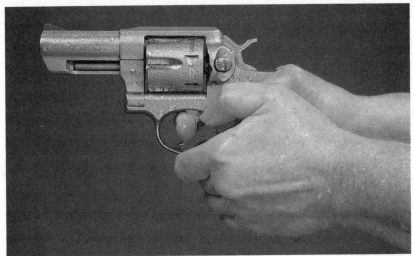
Environmental conditions - like being wet or cold - also affect your balance of speed & precision.

Your anticipation of the need to shoot

Many years ago I was helping out on a hunt for a rabid bobcat at a local farm, sitting in a tree stand carefully surveying the area from which the varmint would likely appear. Everything was ready; my rifle was in a position from which I could easily and without much movement bring it to my shoulder and fire. I'd been careful to make only the slightest and slowest movements with no sound. I was ready for anything, or so I thought.

I'd been there for nearly three hours when, out of the extreme corner of my eye, I saw a flash of movement in an open area well to my right. As I reflexively turned my head to check, I came face to face with the snarling animal on the ground below me and perhaps ten yards away.

I've hunted all my life and have never experienced "buck fever" or any other sort of performance anxiety, but this time I was surprised by an animal that I was, frankly, scared of (a rabid animal being something with which I'm not at all comfortable!). I instantly realized that, in its demented state, it could easily leap to my position and do significant damage to my person. I brought my lever action rifle to my shoulder, clumsily cocking the hammer on the chambered round, and as the butt neared my shoulder I quickly - too quickly - fired the shot. One round, one hydrophobic carnivore. The hit was a good one, but it wasn't exactly where I intended it to go. The mercifully quick kill was as much luck as skill.

By any standard I was ready to shoot; I was on a hunt, had my gun loaded and chambered, had set myself up for the fastest and easiest shot, and was aware of the area the animal should have been in. What I wasn't ready for was that particular shot under those particular conditions. My anticipation of the shot that came was low, even though my general state of readiness was high.

This anticipation of which I speak is the likelihood, in your mind, of having to shoot just before you recognize the need to shoot. You might be ready, you might have all kinds of general awareness, you may even have your revolver in your hand and prepped to stroke the trigger, but if the need to shoot happens in a different place or a slightly different time or under different conditions, your anticipation is low.

When you don't know that you're going to need to shoot, it takes longer to generate the proper response.

This is very different than competition shooting, for instance (which we'll talk about in a little more depth in a later chapter). In a shooting competition, the anticipation of the need to shoot is quite high - you know what the targets are, where they are, how far they are from you, and a number of other things. In that case your readiness and your anticipation are roughly equal, and it takes less time for your mind to generate your response.

Now put yourself into the kind of ambush attack we've been considering throughout this book: you're trying to decide between mocha and espresso when you're suddenly attacked. Your state of general readiness is low, but your anticipation of the need to shoot is even lower. Unless you've trained under that kind of condition, your mind will take time to direct your response.

Your anticipation of the need to shoot - of needing to make any one shot - will therefore have a profound effect on your balance of speed and precision. In my case, I fumbled what had been a well-rehearsed cock-shoulder-fire sequence; I didn't get a perfect cheek weld and I fired before the gun was well anchored on my shoulder. The shot worked, but the deviation was more than I had expected. The low anticipation of the need to shoot, even with my high state of readiness, had dramatically affected my balance of speed and precision. If the animal had been a little further away I might have missed him entirely.

The anticipation of the need to shoot is as much a caution as it is a training prescription. It's easy to practice a choreographed drill on the range and turn in blistering performances. When you know ahead of time that you're going to be shooting a specific shot your brain is primed for the performance; it knows what neurons to fire to get which muscles to do what tasks. When you don't know that you're going to need to shoot, when your anticipation is low, it takes longer to generate the proper response and that response is likely to not look like that well-rehearsed danced on the range.

This idea ties into the confidence issues we talked about earlier. Pretending that you're always ready because you've done the same old predictable drills over and over, and done them really well, is ignoring the reality of anticipation. In the chapter on practice we'll talk about ways to spend your range time getting used to responding better when you're not in anticipation.

Chapter 14

EYES AND SIGHTS
THE DEFENSIVE SIGHTING CONTINUUM

Shooting against another competitor, no matter how seriously, does not produce the same physical reactions as dealing with a predatory attack.

It's normal for the vision to focus on the threat when surprised by an attack. Your technique should take this into account.

Missing from the last half-century of defensive shooting education has been an understanding of how our visual systems work, particularly when in a threat response. This has lead to defensive shooting students expecting to be able to do things that are unlikely to happen when actually facing a lethal attack.

Much of this centered on the idea that, because such things work in competition, mano-a-mano, they must work in a fight. Perhaps this is true in the kind of altercation where the violence is mutual (or at least anticipated), but the body's natural reactions make this highly unlikely when faced with the kind of sudden threat which activates them.

CHANGES IN THE VISUAL SYSTEM

In the chapter on the body's natural reactions, I touched on the changes to the eye: an increase in resolution in the center of the eye and a corresponding increase in image detail to the visual cortex. The 'why' should be obvious: to better see our threat.

Humans are visual creatures, and especially so when we're dealing with something that wants to harm us. Even in those cases where we achieve our initial startle reaction as a result of an audio stimulus, it's our vision that gives us the information about what the threat is doing that allows us to protect ourselves.

That's not the only thing that our bodies do to help us out. Along with increase in resolution comes a locking of visual focus on the threat. The eye locks its focus at optical infinity, which is roughly six meters, and becomes less able (or completely unable) to change focus at will.[21] This combination of focus and resolution serves to fixate attention on the threat - which is exactly where we want and need it to be.

Given these very real physical changes, how reasonable is it to expect that you'll be able to focus precisely on a one-eighth-inch-wide piece of metal being held at arm's length? I'd say, not very!

How then should you practice in anticipation of the changes in your visual systems? By using your eyes the way they've evolved to function: focused firmly on the threat.

FOCUS ON THE THREAT, NOT ON YOUR SIGHTS

Your visual system wants to focus on the threat to gather all the information it can to help you survive. Let it! Focus on the threat - in practice or training, your target - and simply bring the gun into and parallel to your line of sight.

Most people, at the most likely defensive shooting distances, will have no problem getting high-center-chest hits, reliably and at speed, by simply doing this. Again: focus on the target, keep focused on the target, and as you do that simply extend the gun into and parallel with your line of sight. When the gun reaches full extension, stroke the trigger smoothly and swiftly. Make sure that you're using the natural, neutral stance, that you have equal extension with both arms, and that you have the strong, 'crush' grasp covered earlier.

By doing this you're using two methods of aligning the gun on target simultaneously: kinesthetic alignment, where you're physically orienting the gun onto the target, along with a non-cognitive visual component that encourages you to do things that are nice and symmetrical: in other words, parallel.

Orient to the target, focus on it, and bring the gun into and parallel to your line of sight. It's not hard, and it works - even people who have never fired a gun before can easily get vital zone hits, at 12 to 15 feet and in rapid fire, after less than a minute of instruction. I've done it with students and I've seen others do it with theirs. This technique is intuitive, because it works well with what the body does naturally.

This is most assuredly not 'point shooting' in the sense that most people use that word. The gun is being indexed by the natural interaction of your visual line of sight and the mechanical alignment that your equally extended arms provide. Just because you're not using the little pieces of metal on top of the revolver doesn't mean you're not solidly indexing on target.

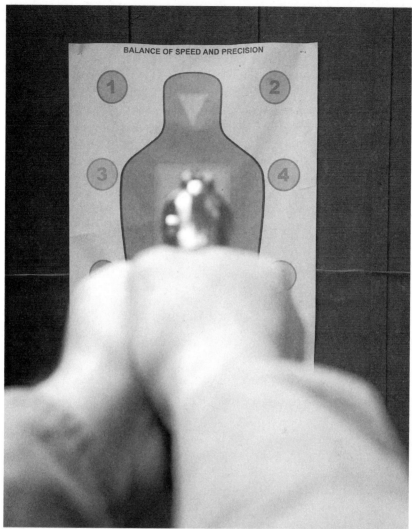

Start by focusing on the target and simply bring the gun into and parallel with your line of sight.

EXTENDING YOUR REACH

How far can you shoot effectively with this technique? It varies from person to person; you'll be different than me, and you won't know until you try. You need to train at varying distances, with varying sized targets, to find out what your limits are. In principle, however, as the precision required increases you'll need to apply more control over the deviation of your muzzle: you'll need to hold the gun steadier, slow down, and pay more attention to a smooth trigger stroke.

There comes a point, however, when the maximum amount of deviation control you're able to apply isn't sufficient to do the job without increasing the precision of your alignment. As it happens, your gun has precision tools built in that allow you to do this - they're called sights.

A sight is nothing more than an alignment guide. There's nothing magical about the sights on your revolver; they just help you align the gun on target. If you're a woodworker or a mechanic, you know all about alignment guides. They serve as handy references to help you put things together more precisely than you could by 'eyeballing.' Sights do the same thing.

I say this not to be overly simplistic, but rather to put you in the right frame of mind. For too long handgun sighting has been taught as an arcane art, one that you mastered only after learning the proper mantra and doing lots of gun kata. Get that out of your head: sights are nothing but alignment guides, and they have a range of use from coarse to fine.

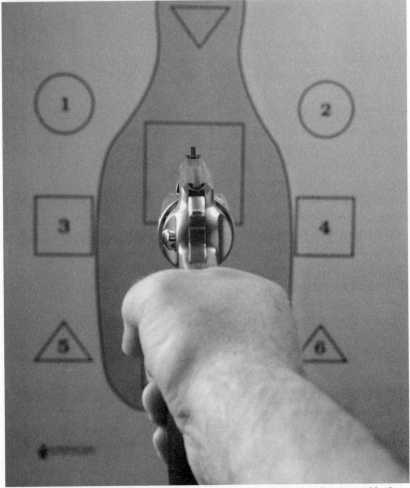

Sights exist to help you more precisely align the muzzle on target. They're alignment guides in the truest sense of the word.

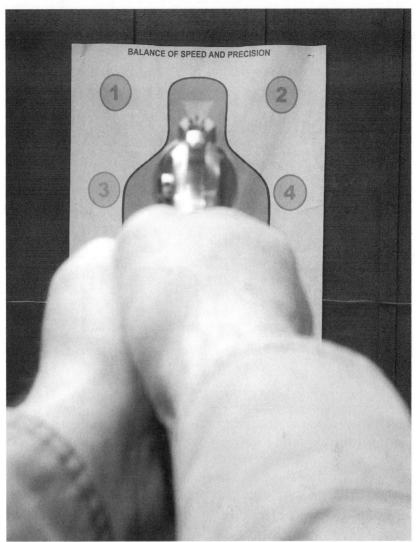

BALANCE OF SPEED AND PRECISION

Focus on the target, let the sights blur - they'll still work to align the gun!

You're looking through the sights, not at the sights.

Once you've found the limits of your ability to align the gun on target by simply bringing it into and parallel with your line of sight, it's time to bring those alignment guides into play. Just as before, you're going to use that natural stance, keep your focus on the target, and extend the gun into and parallel with your line of sight. This time, though, you're going to take notice of your sights.

Note that I didn't say "focus on your sights" - I said, and meant, take notice of them. Your focus will remain locked on the target, just as the clinical and

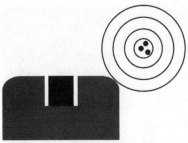

Put the blade inside the notch, with the tops level and an equal amount of light on either side.

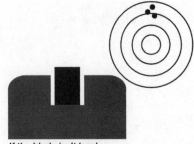

If the blade isn't level, you may shoot high . . .

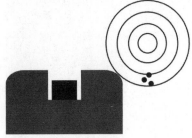

. . . or you may shoot low.

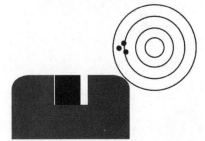

If you have more light on one side of the notch than the other, you'll shoot to the opposite side.

empirical evidence suggests it will - but you'll be deliberately aligning your front and rear sight onto the target. You'll simply superimpose the front and rear sights over your razor-sharp target. You're looking *through* the sights, not *at* the sights.

Your sights will be blurry and the target will be sharp. Don't worry, the alignment guides will still align, and with far better results than the traditionalists will ever acknowledge.

Sight alignment

Let's take a moment to review how to use those alignment guides.

Unless you've done something absolutely wild with your revolver's sights, you'll have some sort of a blade at the muzzle and some sort of a notch at the rear of the frame. Using them is simple: put the blade inside the notch, with the tops level and an equal amount of light on either side.

If the blades aren't level with each other, you'll shoot high or low. If you have more light on one side of the notch than the other, you'll shoot to the opposite side.

Normally, the bullet will hit at the top edge of the front blade. If it doesn't, adjust your sights or change your ammunition - the middle of an attack is not the time to try to remember if your gun shoots high or low.

Proper sight picture

So, what does this focus-on-the-target sight picture look like? The target is sharp, the sights are slightly blurry - but aligned. That's the key. Stay focused on the target as you align the sights and superimpose them on the place where you want to hit, then stroke the trigger smoothly.

The traditional method is to focus sharply on the front sight, align it with the rear, and superimpose the sharp sight picture onto the target. I don't deny that this is the best way to get highly accurate results, as long as a) you can in fact focus on the front sight and b) the target is of sufficient contrast to make the superimposition accurate.

As I've already mentioned when talking about the body's natural reactions, what science tells us in regard to our eye's performance under a threat reaction makes it unlikely that you will be able to focus on that front sight. There are also many people (like me) who can't do so without special glasses. If you're one of those people who wears multi-correction prescriptions, you'll probably be physically prevented from focusing on your sights even if your body would allow it.

In addition, low contrast between the sights and target can make the super-imposition error greater than it would be by focusing on the target.

If you have the eyesight, it's occasionally helpful to practice with a traditional front sight focus to remind yourself what a good sight alignment looks like. My firm belief, however, is that all of your actual defensive shooting practice should be done with a target focus, with or without the addition of the alignment guides we call sights.

SO, WHEN DO YOU USE YOUR SIGHTS?

Simply put, use your sights whenever you need to. Note that I didn't say whenever you *can*, but when you *need* to. It may not seem like much of a distinction, but it is.

Unless I did something extremely choreographed and unrealistic, there's really no training drill that I could give you where you couldn't use your sights. On the training range you've got full control of your responses, capabilities and faculties - nothing is interfering with your eyesight, no one is shooting at you. Under those conditions it's almost impossible to not use the sights.

During an attack, the body's natural reactions cause your eyes to stop ac-commodation – the changing of curvature to focus at different distances – and lock their focus on the threat. This makes it highly unlikely that you'll be able to focus on that narrow piece of metal at the end of your arm. If you can't do that, you can't use those sights as traditionally taught. There is, therefore, a gap of ability between what you can do in practice and what you can do when attacked.

Training to use your sights whenever you can - which on the training range is always - and then getting yourself into a situation where you can't, is a prescription for inferior performance. Instead, practice using your sights only when you need to, when you need the additional precision that the alignment guides on the top of your revolver give you. If you're getting the hits you need to get without them, there's no reason to be using the sights.

SIGHTS AND EFFICIENCY

Remember that your goal is to be efficient. Using the sights in any manner will take a little more time than not using them. If you're spending time using the sights when you don't need to, that time is wasted - you are being inefficient. Not using your sights when you need to means inaccurate shots, which is also inefficient. Using your sights only when you need to is the most efficient method.

In practice, 'whenever you need to' means whenever you recognize (see the 'expert' concept coming in again?) that you can't achieve the level of precision dictated by the target without them. This means, again, that you'll need to train with various target sizes at various distances, preferably called at random by a training partner, and default to not using the sights until you reach failure. When you can't achieve the precision you need with the default, then you bring your sights into play.

Practice to failure, then change something to fix the failure. That's the only way you'll really learn when you need to use your sights - or anything else in defensive shooting.

THE MYTH OF EYE DOMINANCE

A staple of defensive shooting courses is the test to determine your dominant eye, then a prescription of what to do if - like many people - your dominant eye and dominant hand don't match. Usually this test involves some variation of focusing on a distant object, framing that object with your hands, and bringing your hands to your face while keeping the object in clear view. The eye over which your hands land is your dominant eye.

It's common, it's misunderstood, and it's irrelevant to defensive shooting.

A bit of knowledge goes a long way. You have a dominant eye only because your brain has become accustomed to using one eye, the dominant one, for precise X-Y positioning and your other, subordinate, eye for z-axis (depth) information.[23, 24, 25] This preference doesn't appear to be a function of physiology; it's just habituation, and as such it's possible to retrain your brain to make the other eye dominant, then switch back (I've done it myself).

The use of the eyes in a dominant/subordinate manner is how we see everything, how we gather all our visual information, and - most importantly - how we use tools. Our brain expects to see X-Y-Z information, and it puts that information together to form a three-dimensional image. Evolution has produced a visual system of tremendous ability that has facilitated not just

If you've ever done this in class, it may be a sign that you weren't training in realistic defensive shooting skills.

our survival, but our progression as a species. Without it, man would not be a tool-using animal.

The gun is a tool, and the brain expects to be able to use it like any other tool.

When you use a hammer, do you focus on the hammer head and let the nail go blurry? How about putting a key in a lock - do you focus on the tip of the key as you bring it to the keyhole? The answer in both cases is no; you'd find it insanely difficult to hang a picture or open your front door if you did.

We use tools (this is going to sound very familiar) by focusing on the endpoint of the task, putting it in the middle of our line of sight, and bringing the tool to the work. This is how we've evolved to use tools. That is how our vision works naturally.

When under the full force of a body alarm reaction, your visual system is unlikely to operate counter to the many thousands of years that has produced it. It is going to work as it always does, only now it won't be possible to voluntarily change it the way you can when practicing at the range. The body's natural reactions that occur as a result of the threat response ensure that the eyes work the way they've always worked - the way they want to work.

YOUR EYES AND YOUR SHOOTING STANCE

Being intuitive means using the tools of defense, your revolver, the way that your body works naturally, in this case by focusing on the target. It also means bringing the gun into the center of your field of view and parallel with it.

If you adopt a shooting stance in training that brings the gun off-center, your visual system no longer works naturally. Instead of the gun being in the center of your field of vision where your eyes can work together naturally, the gun ends up in front of one eye. The brain can no longer put together the X-Y and Z-axis information, and one eye produces a picture that the brain can't integrate properly. If the dominant eye is not behind the gun, you won't be able to properly align the sights on target unless you close it - or do something else completely non-natural, like craning your neck at a severe angle to compensate.

Once-popular bladed/bent elbows stances bring the gun out of optical alignment with both eyes and are non-intuitive by definition.

These off-center stances are non-intuitive because they don't work with your body's natural reaction of squaring to the threat, or your body's natural use of dominant and subordinate binocular eyesight. Focusing on the target, with a natural stance that puts the gun in the center of your field of view, is intuitive because it all works with how your visual system operates.

This is why the very tests that show you which is your dominant eye also show why it's unimportant: because you have to force your visual system to do something that it's not used to doing, something non-intuitive - which only proves that it doesn't work well that way.

This, I believe, goes a long way to explaining why, regardless of prior training or experience, we consistently see people on surveillance videos adopting the squared-off, neutral stance with both arms extended directly in front of their face. It's the way their bodies - including their visual systems - want to work. Why fight city hall when you don't need to?

Chapter 15

DRAWING THE REVOLVER

M ost people think of the drawstroke in terms of getting the gun into action as quickly as physically possible. There are trainers who have said that the first person to get his gun out of the holster is the winner; many people spend inordinate amounts of time working to perfect the draw, to shave tenths of a second in order to beat a shot timer.

To a large extent this focus on sheer speed of the draw is an artifact of

Just because something can be measured doesn't mean it's important to measure!

an overly competition-based approach to defensive shooting. The draw is something which can be timed, is too often timed, and thus commands more attention than may be appropriate.

As I said in an earlier chapter, very often in videos of actual attacks it's not drawing the gun which appears to waste the most amount of time - it's the decision-making which leads up to the initiation of the draw.

None of the foregoing should be construed to mean that you should bring the gun out of the holster leisurely; quite the opposite. It's only that the draw needs to be kept in perspective given all of the other things that factor into your response.

REMEMBER CONSISTENCY?

The draw stroke should be consistent with all of your other gun-handling skills. Remember when I said that consistency is a big part of efficiency? The drawstroke is a good example.

The physical part of the draw begins with getting a solid, firm grasp on the revolver. If you have covering garments, sweep them out of the way to allow your hand to grab the grip of the gun without getting anything caught.

There many techniques suggested to move clothing out of the way, but I'm not going to ask you to over-think it. Simply figure out how to get your hand

Figure out how to get your hand to the gun without grabbing any clothing along the way, and do that.

Once you have that grasp, lift the gun straight out of the holster. Bring it as far out of the holster as is comfortable

to the gun without grabbing any clothing along the way, and do that. Use your other hand, if necessary, to help you get the garments out of the way. Think not in terms of what to do with the clothing, but simply how to get your hand to the gun. I've found that students figure this out much faster without me introducing convoluted, choreographed maneuvers.

Once you have a solid grasp on the gun, defeat any retention mechanisms that your holster might have. I'm personally not a big fan of retention holsters for a concealed revolver, but if you are that's fine; just be sure to practice smoothly unlatching or unsnapping or un-whatevering the thing as part of your draw.

Once you have that grasp, lift the gun straight out of the holster, parallel to your body so that you are not pointing it at any part of yourself. Bring it as far out of the holster as is comfortable; you don't need to do tendon damage to your elbow, just bring it as far out of the holster as you are able to comfortably.

At this point orient the gun (point the muzzle) directly toward the target. You'll notice that you're now in a position that's very close, if not identical, to the high compressed ready position described earlier.

Here's where consistency comes in. If you've been practicing your grasp and extension, you're already accustomed to presenting the gun from this position. Your draw stroke is now automatically integrated with that part of your

Orient the gun directly toward the target; you're now in a position that's very close, if not identical, to the high compressed ready position.

practice, and you'll see in the chapter on dealing with multiple threats how this integration proves useful.

Once your revolver is oriented on target, simply extend it into and parallel with your line of sight. You're now ready to shoot, or to take the additional time and effort to use your sights.

Practice this in discrete steps first, then make it one continuous movement. Slowly at first, concentrating on where the gun is going; you'll find that you speed up naturally as you get used to the movements. Don't try to go faster until you can do it without error, without fumbling, and without pointing your muzzle at your own body.

This consistency in presentation keeps you from making a draw that messes with your ability to get the gun oriented on target. If you come out of the holster and make a bee-line to the target, you're back to the problems we talked about earlier; the gun is coming up into your field of view at the same time you're reaching extension, which forces you to track the gun visually and stop its upward movement, then correct the inevitable over-shot to bring the gun back into alignment with the target.

If instead you practice the drawstroke as a logical development of the extension, you'll come out of the holster into the high compressed ready, then extend on the target - all in one fluid movement that automatically puts the

Once your revolver is oriented on target, simply extend it into and parallel with your line of sight.

As you initiate your draw, simply take a large step, moving at least one body-width to one side. If you can move more than one body-width in one step, so much the better.

revolver in a line that is parallel with your line of sight. The gun is already aligned on target, and all you have to do is reach extension; it's already there and waiting for the trigger stroke.

The key is to draw the gun through the high compressed ready and extend on the target.

FREE TIME TO DISTRACT YOUR ATTACKER

The drawstroke takes time. Not a lot of it, of course, but it's time that you could be multi-tasking in a way that would keep you safer.

If your attacker is facing you, and you move very rapidly to one side or the other, he'll need to shift his gaze to track you. Human tracking of rapid movement is very complex, but revolves around the brain trying to keep the target centered on the fovea[22]. If the movement is rapid and of sufficient angular distance, the brain has to first catch up then stop itself from over-correction[23]. This all takes time, and if the target stops suddenly it causes disruption in the brain's ability to predict where the target actually is going to be.

It's not a lot of time or a lot of disruption, mind you, but it does happen and you can take advantage of the phenomenon to help affect your attacker's ability to present a lethal threat to you. As you initiate your draw, simply take a large step at right angles (perpendicular) to your target and move at least one body-width to one side. Make the movement very rapidly, and if you can move more than one body-width in one step, so much the better.

Your attacker's brain has to react to your sudden, unanticipated movement, figure out where you're going, direct his eyes to catch up to you, and then react all over again when you stop suddenly. That's activity during which he can't as easily be hurting you.

Again, it's not a lot of time - but in your case it's free! You're already using that bit of time to draw your revolver, and if you move at the same time you draw this slight

Bringing the gun up out of the holster from an appendix position. Note barrel is parallel to the body for safety and shooter is careful not to bring the muzzle higher than the hand that is pulling the covering garment away. (Holster courtesy of Crossbreed Holsters.)

Once the gun is out of the appendix carry, orient the muzzle to the threat. Note that the gun is on its side, but the muzzle is on target.

As the arm extends, wrist rotates to bring revolver into upright shooting position.

distraction ends up costing you nothing.

Do not be mistaken: this movement on your part is not going to magically keep him from shooting or stabbing you, but it's going to make doing so a little harder. Looked at in financial terms, you've made a tidy profit without spending a cent.

When you practice drawing your revolver, move rapidly off the line of attack as soon as you initiate your draw stroke. Make sure that the movement is very sudden, that it's at right angles relative to the target, and that it's at least one full body-width - more if possible.

Some trainers call this "getting off the X," but in this book I'll refer to it as "lateral movement." You should integrate lateral movement with your draw-stroke every time you're on the range practicing or training. Remember the old adage - free is a very good price.

SPECIAL CASES

When dealing with drawstrokes where the gun is other than on the hip, it's useful to go back and pay attention to the basic concepts: draw with the bore-line parallel to your body so that you're not pointing the revolver at yourself, then orient the muzzle directly toward the threat.

Appendix carry

Appendix carry is a good example. Appendix carry, where the gun is inside your waistband between your navel and hip, is getting very popular. It's quite fast to access and is very concealable (if one's wardrobe allows it).

As the revolver comes out of the holster, keep it pointed straight down and parallel to your abdomen. This requires you to bend your wrist rather severely. Now rotate the gun directly toward the target: if you're a right-hander, this means rotating your wrist and fore-arm counter-clockwise. The revolver will now be on its

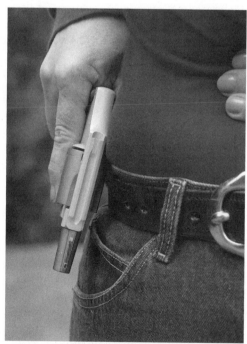

When drawing from a pocket, pay attention to the angle of your muzzle and your leg when the gun comes out; make sure barrel is parallel to leg and not pointing at your foot.

side with the muzzle pointing at the target; simply extend as you bring the gun into and parallel with your line of sight. As you do so, your wrist and forearm will now rotate clockwise back into a normal shooting position.

The same general procedure is the same if you choose to carry in a cross-draw manner. Cross-draw is really nothing more than appendix carry on the weak side, and the same concepts apply.

Pocket carry

Drawing from a pocket isn't all that different from drawing from a belt holster. As you reach into your pocket make your rapid lateral movement. This will usually result in your leg being at an angle to your body, and the tendency is to draw the gun out and orient it vertically as you clear the pocket. If you do so, the muzzle will be pointed toward your leg! Remember: keep the gun parallel to your body. This means keeping the gun at the same angle as your leg until you get it oriented on the target.

I find that moving toward the side on which your gun is pocketed tends to result in a less severe angle and an easier draw as a result, but you need to practice moving to either side. Get used to thinking about keeping the gun parallel until it has become a habit.

PRACTICE THE DRAW FROM REALISTIC POSTURE

At the moment you decide to draw, your body's natural reactions are all but certain to have been activated. You've had a flinch response where your hands have started moving toward your head, you've oriented (physically/visually/mentally/emotionally) toward your target, and your center of gravity has dropped to put you into something resembling a shallow crouch. These are the circumstances under which your drawstroke is likely to happen.

If that's the case, how much sense does it make to practice drawing your gun while standing straight up? Unless you've got some warning about the impending attack (in which case why are you still there?), you're quite un-likely to be standing perfectly erect while you drawing your gun. Instead you should be training under the conditions you are likely to be when attacked: hands somewhere between your waist and your head, knees bent, body weight forward, squared off to the threat.

This is part of realistic training. Training and practicing your techniques under circumstances in which you're unlikely to find yourself only makes your actual response less sure, less efficient. Realistic training in this case means drawing your gun in as close an approximation of your actual position as possible. Bottom line: if you're standing upright when you draw your revolver, you're not training realistically!

Practicing a realistic draw means doing so from a lowered center of gravity, as you would when actually attacked.

This upright stance, common to competition shooting, is not the position in which you're likely to find yourself when surprised by an attacker. Why practice this way?

HOLSTER CHOICE AS A FUNCTION OF YOUR NATURAL REACTIONS

Whether from natural reactions or trained responses, you should assume an aggressive, forward-leaning posture even before starting to draw your gun. As I've mentioned, if you're serious about training realistically you'll adopt that posture during all of your practice exercises.

If your holster choice is one of the belt-carry types, positioned anywhere other than your appendix, that natural position is going to affect how you draw the revolver, and some holsters don't work well under those conditions.

This is because a gun carried on a belt tends to stay in the same place relative to the hips, regardless of the position of the upper body. The shoulders, which carry the arms, move somewhat independently relative to the hips.

The canted holster works with the body's natural reactions.

The instinctive threat reaction posture we've been studying, with the lowered center of gravity and the upper body lean, moves the butt of the revolver backward relative to the arms. Because the shoulders are forward relative to the holster, you'll have to actually pull backwards to get the gun out of the holster. That's not the direction in which your arm is used to operating, or where it has the most strength. There's also an emotional factor, brought about by the fear response: we tend to want to move the tool toward the threat, not away from it.

If you pick a straight-drop holster, that is one without a forward tilt, it will be less efficient and less intuitive to draw smoothly from this threat response posture. You can certainly make it work on a nice, threat-free range, but what about when your life is really on the line?

In contrast, the forward canted holster - often referred to as the "FBI cant" - will release relatively easily from that forward-leaning position. It doesn't work as well when you're standing straight up, which makes it a design that's not in favor with competition shooters. Under the conditions in which it is likely to be needed, however, it is more intuitive and therefore more efficient.

The canted holster puts the exit path of the gun into line with the position that the body is likely to find itself during an attack. It works better with both the body's natural reactions and your trained responses than the straight holster does.

BEYOND THE HOLSTER

Remember that I said your body's natural reactions affect how and what you train? They also affect what you train with. Any piece of hardware you choose to carry, whether it's a gun or a holster, needs to work well with what your body is going to do naturally.

The revolver fits that criterion very well, because it needs no manipulation other than the trigger in order to shoot. It is an efficient design in terms of being able to react to a sudden threat. The forward canted belt holster is in the same category.

Can you use a straight-drop holster for defensive encounters? People have certainly done so over the decades, but you now know that your hardware choice affects your efficiency. The more efficient your response, the less time that you'll be exposed to danger and the less chance you'll have of being injured - or worse - during the attack.

Don't allow yourself to be goaded into your holster selection based on what anyone else uses. If you understand your body's natural reactions, and understand the resulting lowered/leaning stance, you'll be able to make the proper choice.

Chapter 16

CAN YOU

— OR SHOULD YOU?

Should she draw and shoot?

Note: I am not a lawyer, and the following should not be considered legal advice. You should always seek the guidance of a lawyer in your own area, one who is conversant with the laws regarding self defense and the legal ramifications of the affirmative defense in court, before you make any legal decisions. There are criteria by which you might be judged in your actions, and I highly recommend that you take advantage of any courses that deal with the legalities of self defense in your area to familiarize yourself with them.

In the world of defensive shooting instruction there is always the "what if" discussion: "what if this happens, is it legal to shoot someone?" These kind of hypothetical questions are a traditional part of internet gun forums, to the extent that many of them have sub-forums just for such discussions.

Even in courses devoted to the legalities of self defense, a lot of time is spent examining whether you can or cannot shoot someone. How close does someone need to get before shooting is allowed? What kinds of weapons constitute a threat that would excuse shooting? Big vs. small? Many vs. one? Young vs. old?

Don't get me wrong; all of these questions are valid and the answers are important to understanding the application of law in self-defense cases. Knowing legal concepts, such as the affirmative defense and what burdens it puts on you as a defendant in court, is a vital part of your defensive training.

It's also important to understand that shooting a threat may very well lead to his death. While you never, ever shoot with the intent to kill, you do shoot to stop someone from killing you. Very often the result of that fight-ending action is the death of the attacker. This makes the decision to use your gun a very (pardon the pun) grave one; you may end up justifiably taking the life of another.

JUST BECAUSE YOU CAN, DOESN'T MEAN YOU SHOULD

From a philosophical standpoint, our laws are set up to recognize the reality that sometimes it's necessary to shoot, and possibly kill, someone in order to save your own life or the life of another innocent person. That's the basis of the affirmative defense, which itself is the basis for any claim of legitimate self defense: yes, you shot him, but you had an excusable reason for doing so.

In other words, there are situations under the law where you can shoot someone. That doesn't mean you always should, however. Regardless of any local requirements for you to retreat unless otherwise unable, shooting someone should be reserved for those situations where you really need to, when there is no other recourse.

This isn't a defeatist attitude nor am I saying that you must cower in fear. It is an attitude that reflects the fact that shooting another human being - even a lifetime criminal who is no good to society - will change your life. It will cost you money, time, reputation and friendships. A criminal defense might cost you hundreds of thousands of dollars.

Even if you're cleared of criminal charges, the attacker's family might decide to press a civil suit against you, a common happening in today's world. Again, think tens of thousands of dollars - at a minimum.

Shooting someone should always be reserved for those situations where it's really necessary.

HOW DO YOU KNOW IT'S REALLY NECESSARY?

The legal portions of many self-defense classes teach such concepts as abil-

Things have changed! Has her need to shoot changed as well?

ity, opportunity and jeopardy -
the three criteria by which the
use of lethal force is justified.
You need to know those things
ahead of time so that you
understand fully not just why
you're allowed to use lethal
force, but also some of the
situations where you aren't.

That kind of legal analysis
is not something you're likely
to have time for during an
attack, however. In the heat of
action, instead of focusing on

A self-defense shooting can easily become the most expensive thing you'll ever do - regardless of the circumstances.

whether you can use lethal force I believe it's better to focus on whether you
need to.

It's possible, perhaps even likely, that when you really need to shoot there
won't be enough time to run through the legal analysis that answers the question "can I?" Your attacker appears suddenly, you see a known and articulable
threat to your life, and you respond appropriately. That's the very situation
for which our laws are made: when your life is in immediate and otherwise
unavoidable danger and you must make a decision now.

Knowing ahead of time the kinds of attacks to which lethal force is appropriate, and deciding under what circumstances you would and would not shoot, will lay the groundwork for responding efficiently and appropriately.

Don't misunderstand: you may be legally allowed to shoot at some point. The totality of the circumstances may be such that, as the old saying goes, there isn't a jury in the world that would convict you. You may have met all the legal criteria.

None of that means you should exercise your trigger finger unless you need to. This is why a class in the legalities of the use of lethal force is so important.

THE COURTROOM DOWNSIDE TO "CAN I?"

One of the problems with focusing on the "can I" rather than "do I need to" comes when that jury starts looking at your case. There have been court cases (which you can find in the Journal of the Armed Citizens Legal Defense Network, available online) where someone was legally allowed to shoot his attacker (or he at least believed he was legally justified), but the jury looked askance at his decision.

Focusing on the "can I?" tends to look very much like searching for loop-holes, legal technicalities to get a guilty person off. Whether that's right or valid is a discussion for another book, but in those cases where the shoot decisions weren't clear-cut, the defendants had a much harder time - sometimes requiring more than one trial - clearing themselves.

As I see it, it's a lot easier to defend the claim that "I needed to, and here's why" than it is to defend "the law says I could, so I did." That's why I focus on the should rather than the can.

"IF IT'S A GOOD SHOOT, I DON'T HAVE TO WORRY"

One comment I hear a lot when talking about the legal aspects of self defense is the idea that someone who has been involved in a 'clean' or 'good' shoot doesn't have to worry, because his innocence will shine through to protect him.

If you believe that, I have a bridge I'd like to sell you.

The trouble is that neither you nor I (nor the investigating officers) get to decide what's clean and what's not. This isn't to say that they can't choose to drop an investigation due to overwhelming evidence or lack thereof - they certainly can - but not every self defense case is absolutely clear-cut. There are many instances of legitimate defensive shootings where the evidence wasn't completely clear, those situations then being exploited by a politically-motivated prosecutor. I'll refer you to the back issues of the ACLDN Journal[24], which chronicles several such cases.

Ultimately it's only the trier(s) of the facts - the jury, or the judge in a bench trial - that can definitively declare your case to be clean or not. In my state, a Grand Jury makes the first decision, and if they say it isn't clean, it then goes to trial where you have the opportunity for a jury of your peers to make the final decision. In a trial someone else will be scrutinizing your act of self defense, and you'll be paying a lawyer huge sums of money to present your case in a favorable light.

If you remember nothing else, remember this: what looks clean to you or me may not look that way to a person who doesn't understand self defense. Even if you explain it in detail they may still not understand, especially if they're weighing your explanation against that of someone trying to convince them of the opposite.

If you're the defendant, this is probably how it seems your testimony is being evaluated.

A criminal defense attorney I know is fond of saying that self defense is determined by inches and seconds. What seems perfectly fine to you may be interpreted completely differently by people who are looking at those inches and seconds in great detail and with the dual luxuries of time and undivided attention.

CALLING 9-1-1

It's after the incident that you need to be able to articulate why you did what you did. This is where your education in the legalities of self defense becomes important, as they help you understand why the law allowed you to respond with lethal force.

It's important, whether you shoot or not, that you get your own call into the 9-1-1 center as soon as you can. Though to the best of my knowledge it's not legal proof of innocence, investigators often take the stance that the first person to call in is the victim.

This is particularly true in those cases where a gun was drawn and for whatever reasons shots were not fired. The bad guy gets to a phone first and says you assaulted him with a gun; minutes later your call comes in and you say he attacked you with a rock. Which one is more believable at that moment?

Call into 9-1-1 and first tell them your location - address and important landmarks. Tell the operator that you need the police, that you were attacked, and that the attacker is down and needs medical attention. Then describe yourself - height, weight, clothes, distinguishing features. This is so that officers will be able to instantly identify the good guy when they get on scene.

When they arrive, make sure that you're not holding your revolver in your hand! Either holster it before they see you, or put it down - cylinder open - and step away. The last thing you want is for an officer to get out of his car

Make sure you're the first to call 9-1-1, whether you shot or not.

at a shooting scene and see you holding a gun. They don't see the halo we all believe we wear; they see a guy with a gun and a guy on the ground leaking bodily fluids. This is not a situation in which you want to be.

Tell the officers that you were attacked and that you will "sign the complaint" (the actual legal version of "I'll press charges"). Be sure to point out any evidence (attacker's weapon, signs of a scuffle, indications on your person that you were attacked, etc.) so that it isn't missed in the investigation (or so that it doesn't magically stick to an accomplice's fingers and be taken from the scene. It happens.).

Be sure to point out any witnesses as well. People have a tendency to wander off, particularly if they're of the "I don't want to get involved" mentality. Make sure the officers know who can corroborate your story.

Once that's done, it's time to exercise your right to remain silent. In other words, stop talking! Don't give any more detail about how the incident happened or why you did what you did. Human memory is a fragile thing, especially in the midst of a traumatic incident, and you want to avoid saying anything that might be used against you later. You might think you've made an innocuous comment that later proves to be a large point of contention when it doesn't exactly match the objective evidence or eyewitness testimony.

A good course of action, suggested by experts in the field, is to say something like "I know this is a serious situation, and you'll have my full cooperation as soon as I've had a chance to speak with counsel. I'm sure you can appreciate the gravity of my position." This is likely to pretty close to what those same officers have been taught for those instances when they themselves are involved in an on-duty shooting, and serves as one more indication to them that you are, in fact, the innocent party.

This procedure ensures that you've given them the vital information they need to start their investigation, while at the same time exercising (and protecting) your rights against self-incrimination.

How you interact with the police after you've been involved in a shooting, how you articulate why you did what you did, and how well the forensic evidence is preserved will all be parts of how the jury decides whether you were justified or not. It's in your best interest to not screw any of that up.

MAKE USE OF EXPERT RESOURCES

I'll repeat what I said at the top: I strongly recommend that you get appropriate instruction in the legal aftermath of a defensive shooting. The premier source for educational material on the topic is the Armed Citizens Legal Defense Network (www.armedcitizensnetwork.org).

Famed instructor Massad Ayoob travels the country teaching what is probably the best course available on the legal issues of self defense. Called MAG-20, you can find it on his schedule at www.massadayoobgroup.com. On a personal note, I consider MAG-20 to be so important that I suggest everyone who even contemplates using a gun for self defense take the course.

The foremost expert on the legalities of self defense is Massad Ayoob. His classes on judicious use of deadly force should be considered a "must" if you plan to carry a gun for self defense.

Chapter 17

AFTER SHOOTING
— ASSESS!

You may have heard this before - it's common enough to be almost trite - but you live in a 360-degree world. If you're unlucky enough to need to shoot a criminal attacker, you're going to need to learn to deal with all the other things in your environment that may have an impact on the incident: bystanders, law enforcement, witnesses, other injured people, more threats, and so on.

STEP ONE: BREAK THE THREAT FIXATION AND CLEAR THE FIELD OF VIEW

I've been speaking of the body's natural threat fixation, which is a combination of the physical reactions and the emotional (fear) reactions to a lethal attack. The body wants to locks its vision and its attention on the threat in order to be able to react to it, to protect itself.

Once you've shot and that threat has ceased - probably in the form of falling down - it's time to break that natural fixation and prepare to assess your environment. The first step is to get the gun out of your line of vision, which keeps it from blocking your field of view and removes it from your immediate attention.

Simply bring the gun back to the high compressed ready position you've been practicing. This brings it to a position you're accustomed to, one from which you can extend and engage if necessary (again, consistency!). Make sure that you practice bringing your finger out of the triggerguard and placing it on the frame of the revolver as you come back to the ready.

This also clears your field of view so that you can actually look at your environment. Some trainers suggest that you simply swing the gun from side to side, or slightly lower it and do the same thing. The trouble with those ideas is that the combination of the gun and your arms blocks anywhere from a third to more than half of your visual span.

When your gun is held at arms length, even if slightly lowered, you can't see the ground in front of you; you probably can't see your threat on the ground, where he may still be a threat; you won't see bystanders or witnesses cowering low; and you might not see the police officer crouched behind the water fountain ordering you to drop your gun (and you're pointing the thing at him too!).

Bringing the gun back to the high compressed ready eliminates those problems. You now have a clear field of view, top to bottom and side to side, and you can examine your environment in detail without needing to point the gun everywhere you look.

After shooting, bring your gun back into that high, compressed ready position - clearing your field of view and helping to break the threat fixation.

The commonly-taught lowered ready doesn't completely clear your field of view and is not consistent with any other technique you've learned.

STEP TWO: START SEARCHING

When you assess, you're doing a visual search of your environment. This means that you actually need to look at things and people in order to determine if they are in some way connected to your attack. An assessment is a search, and you can't do an effective search if your brain isn't engaged.

You're going to need to turn your head in order to survey your environment. Keep the muzzle of your revolver under control; I suggest that you keep it roughly pointed in the one direction you know it might be needed again: at your threat.

As you turn your head, make quick mental notes about what you're seeing, and mostly what you need to see are people. You may decide to look for something to hide behind while you reload your gun, or simply to get out of the proximity of your threat. Doing the assessment thoroughly will help you find that cover, but you need to actually see things. A quick look around will only produce blurs.

This is why I say that the assessment is a search. A search means that you look for things, and you actually see and think about what you're looking at.

Don't forget to turn to your other side and check what's over there, too!

STEP THREE: LOOK BEHIND YOU

Remember what I said about the 360 degree world? Now would be a good time to integrate that into your assessment.

You're going to need to turn your head in order to survey your environment. Keep the muzzle of your revolver under control.

A search means that you look for things, and you actually see and think about what you're looking at.

You're going to need to look at the environment all around you, because you don't know where anything is going to be relative to your incident. Something very important, like Mr. Police Officer or another Mr. Bad Guy, could

Don't forget to turn to your other side.

Something very important, like Mr. Police Officer or another Mr. Bad Guy, could be directly behind you.

The assessment is a search - and you can't search if you're moving too fast to actually see anything!

be directly behind you. You need to turn your head all the way around, from one side then the other, in order to truly see what's behind you.

Many trainers and schools teach a watered-down form of assessment, one where you simply wag your head from side to side; not only does it make the world go by too quickly for you to actually see anything, it also doesn't allow you to look at the whole picture. It's not realistic in any manner; don't do it! Look all around, and take the time to actually look at things.

SAFELY, OF COURSE

How do you keep your gun from pointing at things it shouldn't be pointed at while you're doing this? First, keep it roughly on the threat you've just engaged. Depending on your level of torso flexibility you may be able to do so by simply turning your head and shoulders all the way around to look behind you. If you don't have that flexibility (as I get older I find mine diminishing), it's okay to move your feet slightly to allow the shoulders to pivot as necessary.

PRACTICING THE ASSESSMENT

It can be a bit un-motivational to practice this on a range, where you don't have a lot of people (if any) or anything interesting to look at. Give yourself a challenge: look to see if anyone else has come in behind you; look to see if doors have opened or closed; look at the lights in the room next to the range; check to see if any cars have come or gone; or perhaps if birds have landed on the gravel. On any range there are things to look at, if you push yourself to do so.

If you're using a public shooting area out in the forest, say on Forest Service or BLM land as is common in the West, this may be both an exercise and a safety strategy. Many assaults have happened in such areas, and my own state has seen a couple of murders over the years by thugs who followed a hapless shooter into the woods with the intention of stealing his guns. In those areas the assessment is actually useful during practice, making it a two-for-one investment: you get needed practice and you keep yourself safe at the same time!

If necessary, move your feet to allow a full 360-degree movement. Keep your muzzle under control; don't let it follow your eyes!

HOW LONG SHOULD IT TAKE?

One of the questions that comes in nearly every class I teach is, "How much time should it take me to do an assessment?"

The answer is, "I don't know."

The speed of the assessment, how rapidly and thoroughly you examine your environment, depends on the environment itself. If you're in the middle of a largely deserted parking lot with most people some distance away, your assessment is going to move a lot more rapidly than if you were in the middle of the mall with lots of people and furnishings around. If you have more to look at, it's going to take you longer to do the assessment. If you have fewer things to look at, it will take less time.

Assessment is a procedure, not an action; it has a purpose. If we tried to attach an arbitrary time for its completion it would no longer have a purpose other than to make the time. The assessment is a search, but a search with a defined purpose. Practice it thoroughly, and don't give into the temptation to make it a quick head wag or succumb to the notion that it must be completed on some sort of arbitrary schedule.

In a later chapter, we'll talk about using the other half of the assessment process to deal with additional threats in your environment.

Chapter 18

DEALING WITH MULTIPLE AGGRESSORS

In the chapter on assessment I mentioned that part of that process was the search for additional threats in your environment. As you look around and really see what's in your environment, one of the things you're going to be looking for is the presence of someone - or someones - who also intends to do you harm. You're looking for additional threats.

While hard data is difficult to come by, the general consensus in the defensive shooting community appears to be that attacks with multiple aggressors - such as home invasions, sexual assaults and robberies - are on the rise. It's within the realm of plausibility that the attacker you shoot will not be alone and it's necessary to find and, if the circumstances warrant, deal with another.

IT STARTS WITH ASSESSMENT

It's therefore plausible that if you've had to shoot to stop a threat to your life, there might be more than one. This is why the first step in dealing with possible multiple threats is to do a thorough assessment: bring your revolver back to the high compressed ready, breaking your target fixation and clearing your field of vision to allow you to make a thorough search of your area.

Remember that the assessment is a search, and you're searching for more people who pose an immediate, otherwise unavoidable threat to your life. This means that you actually have to look at the people in your environment. Does that person have a weapon? Is he/she acting in a manner that would lead a reasonable and prudent person to conclude that there was an immediate threat to your life? The only way you'll be able to ascertain this is if you actually look at the people around you.

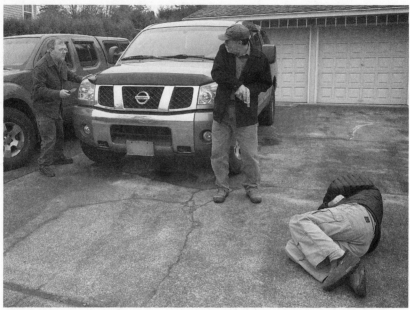

The assessment allows you to locate - and deal with - any additional threats in the incident.

Naturally, if someone is pointing a gun at you or if shots are coming your direction the identification of that threat is probably going to be pretty easy. It might not, however, if all you've ever done is the head-wag scanning technique that's popular in some shooting schools. It also might not be easy if that person is crouched down behind some form of cover. That's why clearing your field of view to do the assessment, and then taking whatever time is necessary (no more but no less) to actually see what you're looking at is so vital.

As you turn your head from one side to the other to do your assessment, make sure that you remember to look at the threat you've already dealt with! He might be getting up to finish the job he started, or might have just enough fight left in him to pull a trigger. He's part of your environment too, and you already know that he's a danger.

WHAT IF YOU FIND ANOTHER THREAT?

So, you're doing a thorough and diligent assessment and you actually come across someone who poses a lethal threat. What do you do now?

Pretty much the same thing you did with the first threat: you forcefully move at least one body-width off the line of attack as you extend your revolver into and parallel to your line of sight and stroke the trigger smoothly until the threat ceases.

If that sounds familiar, that's because it is. What worked for the first threat - what was efficient - will also be efficient for the second threat. If there was something that was more efficient, we'd have used it the first time.

Your learned intuitive response doesn't change, largely because you're body's natural reactions probably haven't changed. You'll still have the natural fixation on the threat, you'll orient toward the threat, your center of gravity will drop and your upper body will lean forward. Since you have a tool in your hand, your primitive grasp reflexes will likely cause you to grip it harder as you're surprised by the new threat; your shoulders may hunch a little as the combination of surprise and sudden grasp pressure tense those muscles.

Those things that work well with what your body does naturally still work.

WHAT DOESN'T MAKE SENSE

If you've taken some self-defense shooting courses you may notice that this method of assessment and response is very different from the typical way that multiple target drills are done, especially in those schools which have a decidedly competition-based curriculum.

In most schools, training for multiple aggressors is done by lining up two or three targets and then practicing firing a certain number of shots at each one. As the students finish shooting the first target, they're taught to move their eyes to the next target as they swing the gun into alignment. This is called transitioning, and is practiced so that the students get faster and faster at the drill.

The problem with this approach is that it only works if three criteria have been met: first, that the student knows ahead of time which targets to shoot; second, that he knows where they are; and third, that they don't move relative to each other.

The problem in our world is that this just doesn't happen. You don't know ahead of time who needs to be shot, because criminals very often flank their victims; in a crowd or a grocery store, you might not even know there was an accomplice.

Even if you did have an inkling that there might be an accomplice, you wouldn't necessarily know where he was. Take a look at some surveillance

camera footage from convenience stores; very often one guy comes in and goes directly to the counter, while the other hangs back and often goes down an aisle where he can keep an eye on things. You wouldn't know if he's to the right or left of the first attacker, and the speed advantage of the swinging transition

The swinging transition technique only works on targets like this.

technique is that you know ahead of time where to look.

Finally, even if you did know at the outset of the shooting who the accomplice was and where he was, it's a pretty good bet that he's not going to be standing still when rounds start going off. Even in the unlikely even that he was standing next to the first threat you engaged, and he drew his gun at exactly the same time (and you knew that), by the time your gun gets out of the holster and you've engaged his buddy Number Two will have moved, out of a well-ingrained sense of self preservation if nothing else. You're going to have to look for him, which brings us back where we started.

The swinging transition technique is based on the idea that you know exactly where you're going to look for the guy you've identified ahead of time, and that he's still there when you get around to him. I've not yet seen solid evidence that this happens with any frequency, if at all.

AGAIN - FASTER DOES NOT MEAN MORE EFFICIENT!

You'll no doubt have people tell you that the swinging transition technique is faster. As pointed out in the chapter on reloading techniques, faster is not the same as more efficient. In the context of a shooting game, the swinging transition technique is certainly more efficient because the very goal is to do it as fast as you can and the environment is set up to allow just that to happen. Since the goal is faster, that technique is more efficient in that context.

In the context of a defensive shooting, it's not as efficient because the conditions are counter to what makes it work in the first place. The targets are moving and thinking, two things which make any technique based on certainty fail, and you have those specific natural reactions that govern how you're going to be able to respond. The result is that you'll need to look for your next threat and, when you find him, you have to deal with him. You have to assess and respond.

Sometimes this assess-and-respond cycle happens very quickly. You see the first threat go down from your shots, and just as you bring the gun into the high compressed ready and start your assessment you find the second threat. He might not be all that far away in real terms (especially in terms of angular distance - degrees), but you still had to locate him. Move laterally relative to him - remember, what was efficient for the first guy is still efficient for the second - as you extend and stroke the trigger.

If you go to a shooting match and start into an assess-and-respond cycle, I can guarantee two things are going to happen: you're going to lose the stage and everyone is going to laugh at you. The context for the assess-and-respond cycle fits the competitive environment no better than the swinging transition technique fits an actual defensive shooting. The context of use is different, and just because they both use a gun doesn't mean they're the same.

This illustrates why you need to train techniques that reflect both the reality of how attacks happen, and the reality of how you are likely to respond to them.

Chapter 19

INTEGRITY IN TRAINING

Integrity (in teg ri ty) - noun
1 - *the quality of being honest*
2 - *the state of being whole, unified, unimpaired, or sound in construction*
3 - *internal consistency or lack of corruption*

In a way, this entire book is about integrity in training to survive a criminal attack: integrity in what you train, integrity in how you train, integrity in your practice, and integrity in you as a student.

Can you train without it? Certainly - many people do, every day. I don't believe that doing so leaves you in the best position to defend yourself, however, and I also believe that it wastes valuable training time. I shouldn't need to remind you, but your time on earth is limited. Why waste it?

HONESTY

Integrity demands that you be honest with yourself. Are you carrying your revolver because you actually have the determination to use it, if it is necessary and appropriate to do so? Or are you carrying it, as so many do, because you feel it keeps you safe but you'd never actually be able to drop the hammer on another human being?

If you're not ready for the awesome responsibility and the possible consequences of using a handgun to defend yourself, be honest enough and don't carry it. To this day I run into new gun owners who buy a gun under the mistaken belief that they can just wave it at their attacker and keep themselves safe. While it's true that the overwhelming majority of defensive gun uses do not involve actually shooting , those instances where shooting is both war-

It's the resolute attitude of the defender which makes her formidable; the revolver just makes her more efficient.

ranted and necessary make it imperative that the gun's owner be emotionally and intellectually able.

Massad Ayoob has famously said that criminals don't fear guns; they fear the resolute man or woman who is holding it. The source of that resoluteness is the defender's honesty with him or herself: that he or she really is willing to shoot if it becomes necessary.

COMMITMENT TO TRAINING

You also need to be honest with yourself about your commitment to training and practice. Are you actually going to seek out training, or are you going to fall back on the "I've been around guns all my life, I don't need to take a class" excuse? The honesty part of integrity is what enables you to admit that you don't, in fact, know all you need to know simply because you had a .22 in the house when you were growing up. (The worst manifestation of this comes from those men who believe that they know everything they need to know about guns simply by virtue of possessing a penis. Sorry for the blunt and graphic comment, but it had to be said.)

Training can come in many forms. While attending a class is, I believe, the best way to train, not everyone can attend a live class with a competent defensive shooting instructor. First, because not everyone who hangs out a

Not everyone can attend a class with a world-class instructor like Rob Pincus, but there are many alternatives to get good training. Start local!

teaching shingle is in fact competent, and second because not everyone lives in proximity to a range where such training occurs.

It's possible to learn from books (like this one!) and videos, but it will take longer, you'll make more mistakes, you won't have informed correction for your errors, and you might miss key points without even knowing. Learning from books and DVDs will take more dedication and attention on your part if you are to get maximum educational value.

COMMITMENT TO PRACTICE

Once you've gotten some training, are you honestly going to put in the practice time to build and maintain your skills? Defensive shooting skills are perishable; they need regular reinforcement through practice in order to remain usable. Practice also generates and maintains the recognition-recall links that are so important to expert-level decision making. Without a commitment to practice you won't retain the skills that you paid to acquire, nor will you be able to use them efficiently.

YOUR COMPETENCY IS YOUR RESPONSIBILITY

Whether you're taking a class or learning on your own, your competency is up to you. The effort you put in, your dedication to understanding the concepts and your willingness to practice - not the parts that are fun but the stuff that's necessary - is what will build your competency.

When you go to a class, be a good student; have integrity. You're there, presumably, to learn something valuable. Pay attention to the instructor, strive to understand the concepts behind what he's telling you, and do what he asks. He may ask you to do something different than what you're used to doing; he may have a new method you've not been exposed to. If you reject it out of hand you'll not have the opportunity to develop competency. Do it his way; if after class you decide that it's not for you that's fine, but while you're there give it a fair shot.

At the same time you should insist that he explain why he's doing what he's doing. His explanations should be reasonable, plausible, and backed by objective data or deductions. If the explanation includes a reference to a famous soldier or police officer or competition shooter without a rational reasoning for the reference, you should ask questions about how it fits into your context. A good instructor should be able to give you the logic and detail to answer your questions.

Beware the instructor who says "try these different ways, and pick the one you like most." Defensive shooting techniques aren't about what you like, they're about what works well with the way attacks happen and with what your body does naturally. You're there to learn what the instructor believes is the best way to do that, and why he believes it to be. If all he does is tell you to pick your favorite, you can do that yourself without spending any money.

Am I saying that the instructor should have a "my way or the highway" approach? To a limited degree, yes. He should be professionally insistent that you put forth some effort to assimilate the techniques he's teaching. You, on the other hand, should really put forth that effort without telling yourself that you don't like it or it's not like the method someone else taught you.

If the instructor asks you why you do something differently than he's asking, you should have an answer other than "that's the way I was taught." If that's the only answer you have, it means your last instructor didn't do a good job of explanation, or you didn't do a good job of listening. It may also mean that your way of doing things may not have a plausible reason for existence. If you find yourself saying "that's the way I was taught," it might be a sign that you need to pay more attention.

At the end of the course, if the instructor has done his job properly by explaining the plausible technique thoroughly and you've done your job by keeping an open mind, you'll have learned - really, truly learned - something new.

BEING WHOLE

The quality of being whole or of being sound means that the training and techniques you learn and practice really reflect and are applicable to your life

Carrying a 5-shot lightweight revolver in your pocket but practicing with a full-size gun on your hip isn't being realistic.

outside of the range - your entire life, not just a piece here and there.

For instance, most people aren't going to do multi-floor house clearing of terrorists in their day-to-day lives. You can find shooting courses, however, where you'll spend a lot of time and money doing exactly that. If that's just not something which actually happens, why waste your valuable resources training for it?

Just about everyone plays several different roles in their lives. There's home, work, recreation, religious observances, and probably a bunch more I'm missing. In each of those roles there are plausible threats, and what is plausible may even change between them. If all you prepare for are the plausible threats in one area of your life, the other areas may not be well covered.

Spending your scarce training resources in doing things that have no plausible use and ignoring plausible skills that might apply to the other areas of your life isn't whole or sound.

This also applies to training with gear - including the gun and holster - other than what you can reasonably expect to use in a real attack. I see many people come to classes and train with full-size belt-carried guns but actually carry a small pocket gun on a day-to-day basis. (The worst offenders come to class with a big autoloading pistol on their belt but actually carry a J-frame in their front pocket during the week!) Part of your integrity as a student is training and practicing with the gear you are actually going to carry.

Yes, I know that you shoot the bigger gun 'better.' Unless you're in that class or on the practice range to impress someone else, that's irrelevant. The reason you train and practice is so that you can get better (more efficient) using the gun you'll actually be counting on to protect you. Discard anything, including your ego, which interferes with that.

INTERNAL CONSISTENCY

In order for your training to have integrity it must be consistent, not just with itself but also with its expected use.

It's not terribly unusual to come across training doctrine which conflicts with itself at some level. When training is based on unrelated techniques that are chosen because they look cool or because some famous military unit used them, you'll often find that they don't work together well. I watched a video of a class where the students were taught to bring their guns up through a ready position, much like I've described, when they draw. When they do their version of an assessment after shooting, though, they drop their guns down without bending their arms, into what has been derisively called the 'urinal position.' When they finish with their rather perfunctory assessment, they bring the gun back up into a high compressed ready, then holster.

That's a lot of wasted movement and, for reasons we covered earlier, is neither consistent nor efficient. Their assessment was likely taken from one school of thought, while their draw stroke and ready position from another. The result was a conflict in action and a lack of internal consistency that resulted in a lot of wasted time and effort.

A higher calling?

Internal consistency means not just that the techniques don't conflict, but that they also work together to support an overall philosophy. Throughout this book I've talked about training in intuitive skills that are efficient under plausible circumstances; everything I've written, I hope, supports that overall view of defensive shooting.

In the Combat Focus® Shooting program, which underlies a lot of my training philosophy, the very description says that it is an intuitive program designed to make you more efficient in the context of a dynamic critical in-cident. Everything that follows during a class reflects back on that statement, supports that statement, and is congruent with that statement. That is a perfect example of internal consistency.

"Tools for the toolbox"

There are things I could teach you that would be a lot of fun and look really cool in a video, but which wouldn't really be applicable to any plausible scenario in your life. Yet, many people do teach such things and use the rubric "another tool for your toolbox" to justify it.

The whole concept of tools for the toolbox is often a smokescreen, a way

"Another tool for your toolbox" is a phrase which can mask a lack of plausible justification for a technique.

to hide a lack of internal consistency. If the only justification for a technique is that it's another tool, that's an indication that it has no application to any sort of plausible scenario, that's it's been included because the instructor is impressed with it for some reason. (That, or he needs to make his students feel that they got their money's worth.)

The toolbox metaphor is also a way for the instructor to avoid conflict; it's a cop-out. It may be that the technique actually does have a plausible reason for existence and that it's valuable to learn. There may be other people in the class, however, who cling to their existing technique because they have an emotional investment in it and won't be swayed by logic. If the instructor doesn't understand why what he's teaching is better and/or lacks the ability to articulate that in a way which allows the student to come to that understanding, then he might fall back on the toolbox analogy.

Whatever the reason, the "tools for your toolbox" comment should be seen as a red flag; an indication that there is little internal consistency or integrity in what's being presented.

Everything you learn needs to have a plausible application. If one exists, then there's no reason to bury it in a toolbox along with a lot of other implausible tools.

Chapter 20
TRAINING IN CONTEXT

Perhaps the most important word in this book, as it relates to the what and how of your training, is the word context. As I mentioned earlier, context means the circumstances or conditions under which something can be fully understood or applied. It acknowledges that there is a relationship between a concept or idea and the specific kinds of situations in which it can be used (or for which it makes sense.)

Understanding context is important because without it, it's easy to make bad decisions with regard to your training. Everything that you learn or practice has a context from which it came, and therefore a context in which it works and makes sense. If the context under which you're likely to use it doesn't match that where it originated, it's possible that it won't be as efficient (or even effective) as it should.

Something which works under one context often doesn't work well under another, but there are situations under which it might. Understanding the context in which you'll use it, as well as that of where it came from, is how you can decide whether it makes sense for you.

THE SHOOTING GAME CONTEXT

Competition shooting has been the source of a lot of innovation in the shooting world, innovation which has migrated to many other uses: hunting, military engagements, and even defensive shooting. That's not to say that the things done in the context of a game are universally applicable to defensive shooting, however.

Some of the advancements in competition shooting are context-neutral. For instance, competitive shooters helped develop the most efficient grasp for an autoloading pistol. For too long, auto pistols were gripped the same as the revolver, and given their very different designs this meant that they weren't being used as efficiently as they could be. Competitive shooters, in their continual experimentation, found the thumbs-forward grip works best for autoloaders - and that is the grip which is overwhelmingly taught by defensive shooting instructors, including yours truly.

The closer a concept or technique gets to commonality between two contexts, the more likely it is to fit. For instance, the grip works in both competition shooting and defensive shooting because in both cases the shooter needs to control the gun while shooting rapid, multiple rounds; the need is the same, regardless of the environmental differences.

Other advancements aren't context-neutral. In the chapter on dealing with multiple threats, I showed you why the competitive 'swinging transition' technique doesn't translate well to the defensive shooting world.

The reason the transition technique doesn't work is because there is very little commonality between the two contexts. The environmental differences (live attackers versus static targets, surprise attack versus known and planned response, performance anxiety versus body's natural threat reactions) and the differences in goals (make good time at all costs versus survive the attack) all serve to make the techniques fail when crossed over.

Even something seemingly simple like using the sights suffers under the environmental variables. In a shooting match, even under the stress of the clock it's pretty hard not to be able to use your sights. In a defensive shooting, the visual changes due to your body's reactions make it physically unlikely that you'll be able to use them. In the shooting match there's nothing to prevent you from using them; in the defensive shooting, your own body doesn't want to work that way. In the former you train to use the sights quickly, in defensive shooting you should train to use them only when you need to - the default being not using them.

THE MILITARY/LAW ENFORCEMENT CONTEXT

While I have been a competitive shooter from time to time, I've never been in the military nor have I been a police officer. That means I'm in no way qualified to talk about how they do their jobs, nor am I qualified to evaluate their shooting techniques relative to those jobs.

Because I'm an avid student of and instructor in the means of surviving the criminal attack, however, I am somewhat qualified to evaluate how applicable their techniques are to private sector defensive shooting. This has been made possible by the large number of their alumni teaching in the private sector, and the material and techniques they're teaching being widely known.

The jobs of those in the public sector (police/military) are different than those you and I have. For instance, in the military their job is to defeat the enemy and take ground (or, as some have pointed out, to kill people and break things). In law enforcement, the task is to apprehend the suspect (hopefully without casualties on either side). In those contexts, doing things like walking toward the enemy/suspect with the gun in a firing position might be a good way to do those jobs. Shooting while walking forward would be a related and thus needed skill.

In the private sector, I can't for the life of me imagine a plausible situation where I'd want or need to shoot at an attacker while walking toward him. This is a skill that public sector trainers often spend quite a bit of time on in their private sector classes, even though it doesn't make a lot of sense in our context.

The same is true for shooting while walking backward. There may be some argument for it in their world (though I'm not sure what it would be), but again in the private sector it doesn't stand up to scrutiny: moving backwards slowly enough to be able to maintain a good balance of speed and precision doesn't really gain you anything against someone with a contact weapon (knife/club), as he'll be able to run toward you much faster than you can backpedal away from him. If he's armed with a gun, there is no physical way for you to move far enough backwards, fast enough, to significantly impact his ability to shoot you.

The idea that you can be ready or proactive is something that comes from a

Shooting while walking forward may have a law enforcement or military application, but for the rest of us it just gives the bad guy more time.

lot of law enforcement training. In their job, it makes sense: they get a call for a man with a knife, and as they head to the call they have the luxury of being able to think a bit about their response and steel themselves for what might happen. When they roll up on the scene they have the advantage of being able to get out of their vehicle while drawing their pistol, ready for action.

In the private sector, as I hope I've shown, the usual incident is a surprise. You don't have any of those luxuries and must instead be able to respond without any sort of preliminary preparation, either mental or physical. Any technique or concept that relies on that sort of proactive posture simply isn't a suitable or realistic way to train for the kind of threats we face - and drawing your gun because you think you might need it is a good way to get arrested.

GOOD TRAINERS, BAD TRAINERS

None of the foregoing is meant to denigrate the earnestness with which some of the competition shooters or public sector trainers present their material, or to suggest that they aren't good at what they do. Some of them do understand the contextual difference between what they do in their 'day job' and what their private citizen students need. Unfortunately, many more do not.

You need to examine what you're being taught and think about whether it really applies to the threats you're likely to face. Shooting while walking forward and backward, for instance, is a lot of fun to do and gives you a great feeling of accomplishment when you do it well. It even seems like they should be valuable skills, but when you sit down and analyze how attacks really happen in our world they suddenly don't seem all that important. That's because they aren't.

I've found that when someone tells me something outlandish is a 'vital skill,' what they often mean is that it's vital to something other than defending from a criminal ambush attack.

DEFENSIVE SHOOTING - IT'S MORE THAN MARKSMANSHIP

Some of the more experienced shooters in the audience probably just had a heart attack, but the fact remains that efficiently defending yourself from the criminal ambush attack isn't just about the shooting. It's about understanding what your reactions will be, learning to make decisions more efficiently, shooting well in relation to the target (as opposed to some arbitrary standard), using intuitive techniques, and so on.

Defensive shooting is about dealing with all the stuff your attacker is doing, all the stuff that you'll be doing naturally, and all of this in whatever environment you find yourself. You're going to have less control than most public sector trainers anticipate, and far less than the competition shooters can imagine. Train under the assumption that you're not going to have full control; if for some reason you find yourself in a situation where you have more control than you expected, you'll be ahead of the game!

Chapter 21

CHOOSING A TRAINING COURSE

It's possible to learn on your own - but it's better to do so under the watchful eye of a qualified instructor.

As I mentioned in an earlier chapter, it's possible to learn defensive shooting skills on your own - but it's really not very practical. While defensive shooting is partly intellectual - knowing when to shoot and why to shoot - it is also somewhat mechanical and athletic, in the sense that you need to do physical things to be able to shoot.

A good defensive shooting instructor will give you a blend of both. He or she should be able to explain the need to process information before, during and after a shooting as well as how to draw the revolver efficiently and put the bullets where they need to go.

EXPERIENCE VERSUS ABILITY

There is a rather vocal subset of defensive shooting students (usually the 'training junkie' type, those whose hobby is taking course after course) who proclaim they'd never take a class from someone who hasn't "seen the elephant." (That's a term meaning to have shot someone. They usually don't make a distinction under what conditions such shootings might have occurred.)

The problem with this attitude is that it's very difficult to find someone who has been involved in a sufficient number of private sector defensive shootings from which to draw appropriate conclusions. I quoted Rory Miller at the beginning of this book as saying that fights are idiosyncratic, meaning that they vary wildly in cause, execution, and conclusion. It's really not possible, except in the most generic sense, to derive a whole lot about defensive shooting from a single - or even two - events. A body of knowledge, of expertise, is only gained from being able to experience a sufficient number of events from which to distill similarities and lessons. That doesn't happen very often, if it ever has, in the realm of private sector defensive shootings.

Think of it this way, every so often you'll find a news report of a completely untrained person who prevailed using a firearm against a criminal despite making every mistake in the book. In other words, he got lucky (as the saying goes, luck counts, but you can't count on luck).

By the seen-the-elephant standard, this guy would be well qualified to teach others how to defend themselves. Would I take a course from someone like that? No. Should you? I can't answer that other than to say it would depend on how much you value your own life.

Virtually all concepts and techniques can be shown dry, with nary a single shot being fired.

The other way that your instructor can learn about defensive shooting is by studying defensive shootings carefully, looking for commonalities and deriving lessons from the mistakes and successes of others. Not having 'dropped the hammer' on someone else doesn't preclude him from learning, for he has the experiences of a wide range of others from which to draw. As Simon ben Zoma said, "Who is wise? He who learns from all men."

ABILITY TO TEACH

In either case, whether from experience or study, the person who can teach is preferable to the person who can't. This is perhaps the most important quality a good instructor can have; no matter how expansive someone's knowledge, if he can't pass that on to his students in a manner that they understand then he might as well not have the knowledge in the first place.

A good instructor should first understand his material at its highest, most conceptual level. He must understand it so well that he can show you how to apply it in the widest range of circumstances. Even though he may only use 10% of that knowledge in any given class, each class may use a different 10%; if his knowledge doesn't go beyond that day's class he'll never be able to answer the questions from the next one. He is teaching beyond his knowledge level and his students will, sooner or later, move past his knowledge. At that point he either stops teaching or starts making things up as he goes along (and I've actually watched the latter happen).

Once he has a sufficiently high level of knowledge he must be able to articulate what he knows. He needs to be able to explain it to you in many different ways so that you can get a well-rounded feel for the ideas behind the techniques. An instructor whose command over the spoken language is poor is going to make a poor instructor, no matter how many times he's 'seen the elephant.'

IS BEING A GOOD SHOOTER A NECESSITY?

There is another subset of training junkies who insist that an instructor be a great shooter, and that he demonstrate his prowess before his students.

A demonstration may sometimes be the most efficient way to get an idea across to students. Language can be slow, but a visual illustration can be very fast. That doesn't relieve the need for the instructor to be able to articulate his ideas, however; a demonstration should be the icing on the cake, not the cake itself.

Note that I never said anything about shooting. Off the top of my head I cannot think of a defensive shooting concept that needs a shot for record (as opposed to a shot necessary to get the gun to operate for some reason). Virtually all concepts and techniques can be shown dry, with nary a single shot being

A demonstration can be a useful teaching tool, but it shouldn't be the primary one.

fired. Stance, grasp and anything else that benefits from engaging the student's mirror neurons can be done without expending a single round of ammunition.

CONTEXT, AGAIN

I've talked quite a bit about context in this book, and picking your instructor or class is another instance where context becomes important.

If your instructor comes from a military, law enforcement or competitive background, it's important that he is teaching things that are really applicable for your day-to-day activities in your office. Just because he's achieved a certain rank, patrolled for a number of years, or won so many trophies doesn't mean that what he's teaching you, if based on his experience, is really applicable.

Again, knowing what's plausible in your life will help you weed out the useful from the useless. The techniques and concepts must match up to your life, must make sense in your environment; if they don't, it doesn't matter how much experience he has. Don't for a minute allow yourself to believe that a uniform or a sponsor's t-shirt means anything to your life; ask questions, think critically.

THE CODE OF THE PROFESSIONAL DEFENSIVE SHOOTING INSTRUCTOR

There is a national organization of self defense firearms teachers, the Association of Defensive Shooting Instructors (ADSI), in whose birth I played a small role. It's composed of defensive shooting instructors from around the country, some famous and others who are only known to their students, who believe in the need for professional instruction in defensive shooting skills. They come together in the ADSI to share, learn, and advance the state of the art in defensive shooting education.

One of the requirements to belong to the ADSI is agreement with the Association's Seven Tenets - a code of behavior, of professionalism, which governs how the instructor teaches, interacts with her students, and relates to her counterparts in the rest of the industry. They're an indication of what the instructor believes and how he/she puts those beliefs into practice, and are what you should expect to find when you choose your instructor.

Tenet #1: *I am committed to the safety of my students, and hold that the expected benefit of any training activity must significantly outweigh any known or perceived risk of that activity.*

We all know that shooting guns in a training environment involves some level of danger. We minimize our exposure to that danger - our risk level - by taking precautions. All safety rules should serve to reduce the risk of the activity, and your instructor should require that all the students follow them.

You as a student should require that your instructor carefully explain all of the safety rules, both the general ones and any specific rules or procedures for certain drills. If you don't feel that the benefits of that drill greatly outweigh the risks as you understand them, you need to ask for clarification. Maybe the instructor forgot something, or perhaps he didn't explain it well; no matter what the cause, he needs to live up to that commitment - and you need to hold him to it. Your life and health, and those of the students around you, depends on it.

Tenet #2: *I believe that it is my responsibility to understand not just what I'm teaching, but WHY I'm teaching any technique or concept, or offering specific advice.*

It's been my experience that a lot of instructors don't really know why they're teaching or recommending something. It usually because they haven't spent a lot of time asking (and answering) probing questions about their material: is this relevant to the student's actual needs? Does it make sense? Is it supported by objective evidence? Is it consistent with everything else being taught? Can it be understood?

The right answer to any "why" question is, "because it's the best thing for the students, and here are the rational reasons which support it." Every technique, every concept, every recommendation has to be considered by that measure. Your instructor should be able to answer the "why" as well (or better) than the "how."

Tenet #3: *I recognize that defensive shooting skills, along with the drills and gear used, are inherently specialized and usually distinct from those of target shooting, competition and hunting endeavors.*

On the chapter about training in context I laid the groundwork for what should now be self-evident: the techniques used in defensive shooting are different than competitive shooting games.

It's not simply about being pro-competition or anti-competition. Your instructor needs to understand what, where and why the differences occur, and be able to articulate them clearly if he/she is to give students what they need. This goes beyond the obvious stuff; it's necessary to understand the nuances, the seemingly little things that actually require big adjustments in curriculum. This only happens if the instructor isn't wedded to one point of view and if he/she really understands what defensive shooting is about.

Your instructor should demonstrate that he or she knows the difference, and can do that by acknowledging to you that there is a difference.

Tenet #4: *I will encourage my students to ask questions about course material, and I will answer them with thorough and objective explanations.*

It's actually very easy to discourage students from asking questions. Think back to when you were in college: how eager were you to ask, in front of people you barely knew, what might be seen as a 'stupid' question? Anything that a student perceives as being dismissive of their questions, or worse belittling of their state of knowledge, will put a damper not just on their desire for clarification - but the rest of the class' as well.

Every student needs to feel comfortable asking any pertinent question, and moreover it's important for the instructor to always prompt for those questions. The students need to know that they can ask even the most probing questions about the material without being made to feel that they're unworthy.

Your instructor needs to give you answers that are complete and based on fact, logic and reason. There should be a good reason - preferably several - for every answer that's given, and they should all be factually based. Of course, they should also be consistent with the rest of his answers and curriculum.

You shouldn't accept flawed logic (like Appeal To Authority), unsupported conjecture or incomplete/out of date evidence. Don't tolerate dogmatic sound bites that contain no fact and serve only to shut down further inquiry.

The professional gives students plenty of opportunity to ask questions. He maintains an atmosphere in which discourse about the topics is not only allowed, but encouraged on a continual basis (once at the end of class isn't enough). The answers to all questions are respectful of both the material and the student, and are based on provable and supportable facts - never mere opinions or sound bites.

Tenet #5: *I understand that Integrity and Professionalism are subjective traits and I strive to maintain high levels of both. I am capable of, and willing to, articulate the reasons for the way I conduct my courses and how I interact with students & peers.*

Your instructor should always be above board - not just with you, but all of his other students and his peers. He needs to voluntarily be accountable to his students and his colleagues for everything he does. He should demonstrably adopt and behave to a high standard, and be open to constructive criticism, especially from you the student, when he comes up short.

Tenet #6: *I believe that it is valuable to engage my peers in constructive conversation about differences in technique and concept, with the goal of mutual education and evolution.*

Being able to talk to other professionals about what he does, and finding out why they might do something different, is the basis of professional interaction. Every professional interaction I've had with other instructors has been an opportunity to learn, even when our approaches were quite different. In each of these I've come away with something that made me a better instructor - if only because it gave me an opportunity to advance my ability to articulate what I do.

How to tell if your instructor abides by this? Listen to him talk about other instructors; if he's throwing rocks or bad-mouthing others, he probably doesn't. There's a difference between respectfully or jokingly needling one's peers and talking trash about them. Professionals talk to each other - they don't throw rocks.

Tenet #7: *I believe that the best instructor is an avid student, and I will strive to continually upgrade my own skills and knowledge. As part of this belief, I understand that my own teachings need to be subject to critique and open to evolution.*

Everything evolves, changes, progresses. It's how we as human beings make progress in any field - and defensive shooting is no exception. We've come a long way even in the last couple of decades, and I'm sure we'll move even further - if for no other reason than to advance our teaching skills. The way the professional instructor does this is to be a student again.

Being an avid student doesn't mean just signing up for another class from his favorite guru, nor does it mean taking a class from someone whose curriculum is largely consistent with his current worldview. It means seeking out new information and different approaches; being open and receptive to new ideas and giving them full (and honest) consideration.

How to know if your instructor is really committed to staying on top of his knowledge? Ask him what he's changed his mind about in the last year: what does he teach now that he didn't twelve months ago, or what did he teach then that he doesn't now? Don't settle for a politician's deflection; if he's really learning and evolving, he should be able to tell you something specific that he either started or stopped teaching. This is really the litmus test for an instructor.

FINAL THOUGHTS

This Code is a description of an ideal, a list of traits that other Professionals agree are desirable and laudable. It's not necessarily always achievable, but your instructor should always be working at it - and should be proud to tell you how he's doing so. There is always room for improvement, for progress, for evolution, and the Professional understands that. He doesn't stand still.

If you're a student of defensive shooting, it is what you should expect of your instructor. If you're an instructor, it comprises the things that you should want to do -- to better yourself, better serve your students, and move the industry as a whole forward.

Chapter 22

PRACTICING REALISTICALLY

In the chapter on making decisions more efficiently I talked about training realistically, adopting techniques that were intuitive and thus realistic, and practicing under realistic conditions to the greatest degree possible. This chapter is about your practice - what you do after you've trained in the techniques so far outlined.

IT DOESN'T NEED TO BE AUTHENTIC TO BE REAL

In the training world we often use the term realistic to mean authentic. For instance, many ranges or schools have shoot houses that are furnished much like your home might be. You'll find bedrooms, living rooms and sometimes even offices (though I have yet to see a bathroom).

The concept is that if you train inside of spaces that resemble something in your world, the training is more realistic. The issue I have with this idea is that just because something looks real doesn't mean it's realistic; unless it duplicates what your home is like, it's not realistic to you - it's just another abstraction but with better props. A much better word for these abstractions is authentic, in the sense that it looks like it could be an actual room somewhere, but it's not realistic because it doesn't represent your room.

This isn't to say that abstractions are necessarily bad or to be avoided. An abstraction that represents your actual world is quite valuable, but one which represents someone else's probably won't be. The key is to consider your world and reproduce enough of it to get maximum value out of the exercise.

YOU NEED A PARTNER

Someone once asked me if I thought it was important to use a shot timer when practicing. I think I stunned the poor fellow when I told him I thought it was next to useless; instead, I told him, the most important thing he could take to the range when practicing defensive shooting was a partner - and that person doesn't even need to be a shooter!

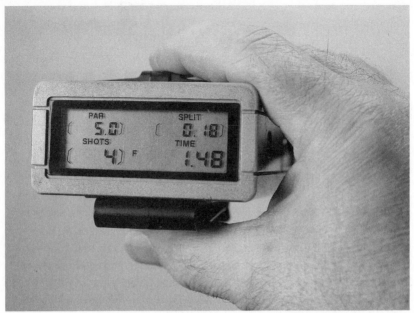

The author's vote for the most useless tool in defensive shooting training: the shot timer.

One of the biggest impediments to practicing realistically and developing your ability to use recognition like an expert is shooting the same thing all the time. You know what you'll be shooting, you know where it is, and you know what level of precision the target demands. There is nothing for you to recognize, which is one of the major points of practicing realistically.

Even using randomizers such as dice (throw the die then shoot the target whose number comes up) isn't enough because you have time to look at the die and figure out what you'll be shooting.

You need an unpredictable, random indication of the target to be shot. With each string of fire there must be options which you face, options which you must process before making the decision to shoot. The goal is to reduce your anticipation to the greatest degree possible. (We discussed the difference between readiness and anticipation earlier; you're on the range, you know you're going to be practicing, so it's foolish to believe that your readiness can be short-circuited. Your anticipation of the need to shoot, however, can be manipulated by your training partner.)

Your partner should be instructed to call different targets - varying in size, color, shape, distance and whatever other variables you can introduce given the limits of the range and your equipment. Use numbers, letters, mathematical symbols or even spelling challenges to force you to process information prior to executing your skills.

A random target call helps you develop your ability to recognize a threat, recognize the precision needed, recognize the balance of speed and precision that is appropriate to the circumstances, and to apply the correct amount of deviation control to deliver the accuracy needed.

Don't shoot the same number of rounds each time!

Imagine this: in five minutes you'll be forced to shoot an attacker who is trying to kill you. How many rounds is it going to take to stop him?

If you answered anything other than "I don't know," you're fooling yourself. (If you answered "one, because I'm such a good shot/use such a powerful round," go to the back of the class and re-read every chapter from the beginning!) You don't know how many rounds it's going to take to cause your threat to stop, and you shouldn't be practicing as though you do know.

When you're practicing defensive shooting you should always practice firing a random number of shots that you choose (or better yet, visualize - more about that in a bit). Sometimes one, sometimes the whole cylinder - but most of the times you should shoot two, three or four rounds. Don't shoot the same number twice in a row, and don't default to shooting the competition-inspired 'double-tap.'

TARGETS FOR DEFENSIVE SHOOTING PRACTICE

If someone folds a piece of paper in half and says "that's a good defensive group, and we're going to practice shooting it as fast as possible," that's not practicing realistically. You have nothing to recognize because the precision needed has been statically and arbitrarily predetermined. The drill becomes a choreographed and overly mechanical test of muscle control, and you end up focusing on the anticipation of the shot as opposed to the recognition of the need to shoot.

The ideal defensive shooting target isn't authentic, in the sense that it looks 'real' (as with the photographic targets so popular these days). It is realistic, in the sense that you're not sure what needs to be shot (or even that you should shoot) until your partner gives you some indication that you need to shoot. This mimics the way that attacks actually happen: you don't know ahead of time what you're going to shoot, or even that you need to shoot.

The I.C.E. Training Balance of Speed and Precision target is illustrative of the concept. In one target are four shapes, five colors, six numbers, three different sizes, two letters and several compass directions. On this one target your training partner can randomize the shooting calls to the point that you can't easily predict what's coming next. In addition there are several targets which are duplicates, allowing you an easy way to practice the assess-and-respond approach to dealing with multiple attackers we talked about earlier. This target is available from www.letargets.com, catalog #CFS-BSP.

Don't think, however, that you need a fancy store-bought target to do these things. Here are some I printed out on my computer. Note the different sizes, shapes and denominators. If you have a color printer (which I do) and live where it doesn't rain (I don't) you can even make them in a variety of colors.

Still too fancy? Simple - use white paper and spray paint.

Spray paint can also augment an otherwise bland target to make it suitable for randomized practice calls. Take a blank IDPA or USPSA target and paint letters and numbers on it. Better yet, take several and mark them all up differently.

It's easy to think that you need some special target to practice defensive shooting skills, but what you really need is imagination. In classes I use the I.C.E. target

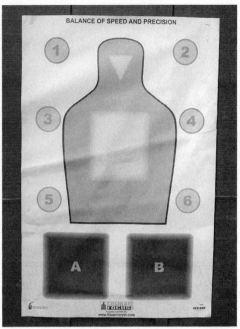

The Balance Of Speed and Precision target, available from Law Enforcement Targets, is an ideal training aid because of the number of ways in which it can be used.

simply because it's efficient in a class setting; we can go through a whole lot of drills before we need to change targets, which saves a lot of time. By yourself, though, that shouldn't be much of a concern and you can avail yourself of the more accessible options.

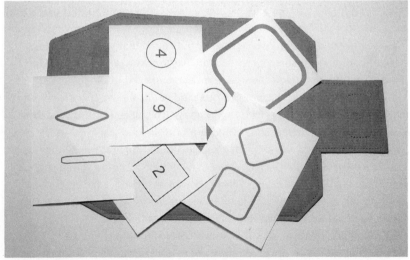

Almost any target can be used, and you can even make your own using simple shapes and your computer printer. (You can download these, and more, at www.grantcunningham.com.)

All you need for realistic training is some white paper, spray paint and a little imagination!

If you choose to make your own targets, either on your computer or just using spray paint, keep these guidelines in mind:

- Have at least one target that approximates the size of the upper-center-chest of an attacker. An 8-inch circle works pretty well, as does a standard sheet of copier paper with the bottom three inches folded under.
- Have at least a couple of shapes, and the more the merrier. A circle, triangle and square are good for starters, and don't hesitate to turn the triangle in different directions.
- Vary the sizes. In general, the smaller targets should be no larger than half the size of the largest (the high-center-chest) target.
- Add numbers or letters (or both!) to some of the targets.
- If you can, adding colors gives you more options. Stick with the primary colors: black, blue, red, green. I've found that lighter colors like yellow

don't show up well enough in many conditions.

• Don't add scoring areas. Remember that the target determines the precision needed; if you desire the chance to shoot with more precision, make the target smaller.

• Don't add "aiming points." Again, the target determines the precision needed; if you can't deliver that level of precision the aiming point isn't going to help, but more deviation control will.

• Don't worry about making perfect shapes or making them identical. This isn't a contest where everyone needs the same 'fair' chance; this is practice at developing recognition and recall of shooting skills. You don't need perfect shapes for that.

VISUALIZATION AS REALITY

There is a large body of evidence, which I'll leave to you to discover, that deals with visualization as a training and practice tool. The neuroscience is still being researched, but the general belief is that the brain doesn't really know the difference between what it sees and what it imagines.

This was brought home to me when my late father was in the hospital for a procedure and experienced a psychotic reaction to his pain medication. In his delirium he said he saw little men dropping wires out of the ceiling and climbing down onto his bed. He could describe the color coding of the wires (he was an engineer for the phone company - he knew his wiring!) and what the little men were wearing. As he told me afterward, they were perfectly realistic - as real as I was, he said. What the mind constructs is as real as what it actually sees.

You can use visualization as a tool to inject realism into your practice. Start by visualizing a threat when you look at the target. Visualize to whatever degree of detail you wish, but some of the variables to consider might be height, weight, sex, ethnicity, facial hair, shirt color, shoes, gloves, headwear, glasses, hair color, tattoos, eye color, jacket, vest, pants, shorts, pant color,

Visualizing a threat when you look at your target is a superb training tool.

shoelace color, rings or watches and anything else you might think of.

The most important part is to visualize those clues that indicate to you that he is a threat: weapons (gun, knife, broken bottle, baseball bat, fencepost, motorcycle chain, screwdriver, etc.) and other indicators of intent like his actions, demeanor, facial expressions and body language.

The key is to make it specific and don't repeat the same person. Make it different every time, lest you latch on to the idea that only certain types of people can be threats. Mix it up, but visualize to the extent that you see more than just your paper target.

Visualize effects

When you shoot, visualize your threat reacting to your shots; after you've fired whatever number of rounds you decide will defeat your attacker, visualize him or her falling to the ground, dropping the weapon or giving up. This helps to reinforce the idea that you don't know how many rounds it will take to stop the attack until it happens, and it also helps to develop your ability to assess the threat as you shoot.

Many people like to follow the target to the ground to ensure that he is really out of the fight. I have no problem with you doing this, provided your whole upper torso is involved. The gun should stay in and parallel to your line of sight as you follow the image of the target. If, however, all you're doing is dropping the gun into some sort of low ready position then don't. The idea of

If you choose to visualize "follow the threat down," do so from a shooting position - don't just lower the gun.

following the target is to be able to immediately trigger a shot if he proves to still be a threat; you can't do that if they gun isn't in a shooting position: in and parallel with your line of sight and fully extended.

If you choose to do this remember that the gun comes straight back into the high compressed ready when you're satisfied that he's down for good; from that position you start your assessment.

Visualizing an environment

A step up from the visualization of a threat is the visualization of space. Here you need to be specific. Visualize things from your life: your bedroom or living room, your office, your bank, the coffee shop you frequent, the mall where you go for your shoes, the parking lot at your favorite movie theater or anyplace else that you've been and might likely be again. Don't forget your vehicles, your desk, or your spouse or children - those are all part of your world as well.

This is particularly important when doing drills, like dealing with multiple threats, in which the environment has a huge impact on what your attackers will do and how you will respond.

The reason you're doing these drills is to cement in your mind the balance of speed and precision you need for various targets at various distances.

It's one thing to shoot a target on a static gravel range; it's another to see a vicious criminal in your local grocery store parking lot attack your wife while you're returning the shopping cart. The beauty of controlled visualization is that it allows you to practice your application of the skills you've learned in the context you'll likely use them. This is a huge aid to building the recognition-recall-response sequence we've been talking about throughout this book.

ARTIFICIAL LEVELS OF PRECISION

There is a practice/training strategy which you've no doubt encountered: the idea that you should shoot to a greater level of precision in practice because you'll shoot bigger groups in a real defensive encounter.

There isn't really a physical explanation for this. Several trainers - the most notable being Massad Ayoob - have experimented with injecting willing subjects of known shooting ability with epinephrine, then having them shoot a prescribed course of fire. In many cases the subjects shot just as well, or very nearly as well, as they did in their baseline tests. The muscle tremors and other effects of a stress reaction don't appear to dramatically affect the physical or athletic ability to shoot.

Why, then, does the idea persist that you'll shoot at half the level of precision in an actual defensive encounter? I believe it's due to not training realistically - under the conditions you're likely to experience.

We often see it in classes when we put people through evaluation drills: exercises designed to test the student's ability to apply their skills in context. For a large percentage of the students, once we've stripped them of the anticipation of the need to shoot and randomize the target calls they tend to shoot with less precision than they do when shooting something familiar. Some of this is certainly performance anxiety, but much of it is simply because they haven't learned what their balance of speed and precision is under the circumstances which are being tested. They guess, and they often guess poorly. Once they get a good grasp of that their performance improves.

It all goes back to confidence in their skills: a large percentage of those students always shoot much more quickly than they can get the hits they need, and they tend not to alter their balance of speed and precision as their relationship to the target changes. They're over-confident because they haven't trained under realistic conditions sufficiently.

I see the opposite as well. Occasionally a student who has trained to shoot ever-smaller groups as a hallmark of defensive shooting will shoot far more slowly than he or she needs to during an evaluation drill. Unaccustomed to doing anything else, these students are under confident of their abilities; since all they have ever done is take their time to make 'perfect' hits, that's what they do when presented with any shooting challenge.

You don't need to practice shooting artificially or arbitrarily greater levels of precision to ensure that you'll be able to deliver a given level of precision on demand; you need to practice delivering an appropriate level of preci-

Students are often confused and reach a failure point when put through evaluations for which they haven't thoroughly trained.

sion, dictated by the target and recognized by you, under varying and random conditions.

The idea is to make the connection between what you recognize and the skills you recall, and that doesn't happen without getting out of your comfort zone of always knowing what you're going to shoot next.

PRACTICE IDEAS

These are some suggested drills that are in accordance with the principles outlined in this book. None of them require more than a simple range (though drawing from the holster and the ability to "rapid fire" are necessary). Most of these are taken or adapted from drills taught to Combat Focus® Shooting students.

General concepts

When your partner calls a target, any target, simulate the natural reactions you'll likely to encounter in a real attack: square your feet and body to the target, lower your center of gravity and lean forward (simply throwing your butt back six to eight inches will usually put you in the proper position), and start to bring your hands convulsively toward your line of sight as you look for your target. When you find it, start your draw stroke just as in the previous chapter: grip and move laterally (at right angles) to the target as you draw. You should be solidly planted - feet no longer moving - when you hit full extension and start shooting.

Don't choreograph your response; don't bring the hands up to a competition-like surrender position, for instance. I tell my students that the correct response should look like a flinch - a strong, convulsive, somewhat exaggerated flinch that is different every time you do it.

You should not be drawing your revolver until you recognize that you have a target. Remember, train realistically: if you're in the mall and you hear a loud noise, are you going to immediately reach for your gun before finding out if there's really a threat? Of course not, but that's how most people train. Don't allow yourself to get into that competition-inspired frame of mind. You simulate the natural reactions, then when you find your target and make the decision to shoot move laterally and draw your revolver.

Unless otherwise noted, the large (high-center-chest area target) is to be shot multiple times; make it a random number of rounds between two and five. Mix them up and don't get into a pattern!

Again, unless otherwise directed, any smaller targets will be one round only - hit or miss, one round only.

You should always be shooting as fast as you believe you can get the hits you need. If you're not getting the hits, slow down; if your groups are nice and small and centered in the middle of the target area, that's a sign that you're wasting

It's an extreme example - but if you haven't identified a target before drawing your gun, why are you drawing at all?

time on meaningless increments of precision; speed up until you start missing.

Reload when you need to; your partner should not need to tell you to reload. When you recognize that you're out of ammunition, immediately reload the revolver. Remember to move when you reload - don't sit there like a target! I suggest having at least three speedloaders or strips on your person to maintain the momentum of the drills.

Balance of Speed & Precision drill

Use a target with at a high-center-chest sized area and at least three smaller targets with numbers or letters in them. Your training partner should be told to make about 80% of the target calls on the large target; you can use any term you'd like, but "UP" and "THREAT" are simple and easy to understand even with hearing protection. Occasionally he should call one of the small targets by number or letter.

The default for this drill is to focus on the target and keep your focus there. Simply bring the gun into and parallel with your line of sight and stroke the trigger. Later you'll make changes to this as you need to, but for now focus on the target and just bring the gun into your line of sight.

Face the target from about three yards away. Have your partner call the target and you will respond appropriately (remember to simulate the body's natural reactions every time, including your shooting stance). As soon as you're finished, re-holster and wait for the next target command. Reload when you need to; do this until you run out of ammunition.

Now evaluate your target. Remember that accuracy is yes or no; you either hit within the target's area of precision or you didn't. Don't allow yourself to devolve into thinking that shots in the center are better than those which are off a bit. As long as they're inside of the target area, they're good - move on.

If you've got a nice group in the middle of the large target, you're taking too much time. Remember the discussion about shooting to a greater level of precision than the target requires? If you're doing

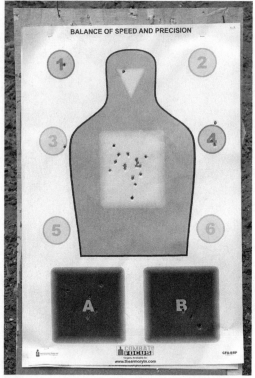

Your partner should call a mix of large and small targets, and use colors, numbers or shapes to help randomize the commands.

that, speed up - take less time. Push yourself to the point that you start to land some shots outside of the target area.

Any shots that land outside of the target are misses; where are yours? On the large target, are the missed rounds on your first shot, or on subsequent shots? If on the first shot, it may be that your feet aren't planted when you start shooting, you're not at full extension, or your grasp is insufficient causing your trigger finger to steer the gun.

If the misses are on subsequent shots it's often a sign that you're not controlling recoil well. First correct any stance/grasp issues - make sure that you're not relaxing your grasp as the trigger resets and be certain that your center of gravity is lowered and your upper body weight is well forward (commonly called "leaning into the gun"). Be sure that your arms are extended as far as possible, preferably with your elbows locked, and that your shoulders are rolled up and forward. If those things don't solve your subsequent misses, then slow down! Slowing your shooting pace will usually bring those shots into the target area but should not be done until you've corrected any and all physical deficiencies.

On the small targets you only have one shot; if you've missed, and you've corrected all of the physical issues I just talked about, it's possible that you need

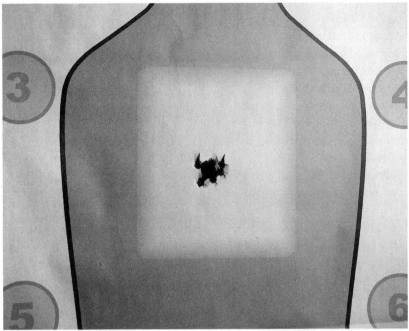

A tight group in the center of an area means you're taking far too much time for the level of precision the target dictates.

to use your sights at this distance and with that size target. On the next string of fire, use your sights if you feel you need to. If that corrected the problem with misses, you now know that on targets of that size, at that distance, you need to use your sights.

If you're still missing it's likely that you have a problem with trigger control. Do some exercises as outlined in the chapter on trigger control, then immediately shoot another string of live fire. If the problem is solved, then try again without using the sights.

Once you've done this several times (say, 70 rounds or so) move back to about five yards and start all over again. You might find that you don't need to use your sights at all at three yards, but at five yards

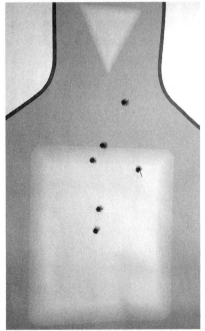

These misses came on subsequent shots, indicating the shooter doesn't have good control - or is simply shooting too fast to effectively control the recoil of the gun.

you need to use them on the small targets. That's fine! You'll likely find that you need to slow down a little bit at this distance; that's fine too. The reason you're doing these drills is to cement in your mind what balance of speed and precision you need for various targets at various distances.

You'll know that you've gotten a good feel for your balance of speed and distance at these ranges when you're always shooting as fast as you believe you can get the hits -

Repeated misses on a small target may mean you need to use your sights or work on your trigger control.

and getting them. When you reach that point it's useful to extend your range just a bit, out to say seven yards. Again, start over and learn where your balance is at this distance. You'll find that you need to apply a lot more deviation control than you did up close, and that's going to slow you down. That's what you want to learn now, instead of when someone is shooting at you.

This is the basic drill that should account for at least half of your range time every time you practice. This isn't a drill that you shoot well and say, "OK, I'm good at that!" It's a drill that's always changing, because your balance of speed and precision will always be changing. No matter how good yours is, it can always stand improvement.

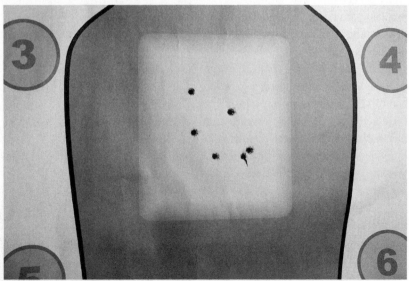

This target shows the shooter has a good grasp of his or her balance of speed and precision under specific conditions.

Information Processing drill

Being able to process information prior to the execution of a learned skill is the basis of intuitive shooting. In Combat Focus® Shooting this is called a "Cognitive Drill" because it tests your ability focus on something other than the shooting.

For this drill you'll need the same sort of target as in the Balance Of Speed & Precision drill, but you'll need to

You can really increase the difficulty of information processing by adding numbers and letters to regular targets.

have some additional options. (This is where the I.C.E. Training target really comes into its own, but again you can make perfectly suitable substitutes.)

You'll need a high-center-chest sized target and several smaller targets differentiated with numbers, letters, shapes or colors (preferably all of these). You can also have a second target stand with a similar but not identical setup - use different numbers, letters, colors or shapes on the second stand.

Your training partner's job is to mix things up for you. Just like the Balance of Speed & Precision drill, most of the calls should be on the high center chest area, but the rest of the calls should not necessarily be immediately obvious. For instance, he might use a math formula ("2 plus 3"). He might say something like, "what is the first letter of 'rabbit'?" (If he really wants to mess with you, he might call, "what is the first letter of 'psychology'?"!) He can call a color or a shape, and so on. If there is more than one target that contains the solution (two or more of the same color, shape or even number or letter) you'll need to do a proper multiple threat assessment-and-response sequence.

Once or twice he should make a call for which there is no solution - just to test if you're drawing your revolver habitually rather than after processing the information. This drill is to develop your decision making and information gathering rather than just blasting away.

This is a drill which really benefits from video. Most people, when forced into thinking about stuff other than the actual shooting, start to revert back to well-trained routines that aren't necessarily intuitive. If, for instance, you've always trained in a bent-elbow Weaver stance and the neutral intuitive stance is relatively new to you, you're likely to revert back to old training when required to do something new - like thinking before shooting. Your training partner can help you with this, but if he or she isn't really up on the subject (or isn't a shooter) you won't get the feedback you need. Video is a wonderful tool to help you diagnose errors.

Moving Point Of Aim drill

This drill was taught to me by Georges Rahbani, a gifted instructor who also happens to be a good friend. It's an old drill, and I've heard it called by many names since first seeing it. (Rob Pincus, founder of I.C.E. Training, half-jokingly called it the "Dynamic Deviation Control drill," and the name stuck. It's actually a pretty good description!)

There are several goals of this drill. First is to impress upon you that no one holds a gun perfectly still, and that deviation control happens continuously as you shoot. It also, ironically, helps you to work on your trigger control by forcing you to think about something other than the trigger. For those who have developed a flinch, I've found this drill to be a quick cure. It teaches you to deliver whatever level of precision you need (based on what the target demands) and I find reasons to use it in nearly every class I teach.

Start with the large, high-center-chest sized target. Your gun should be in your hands, extended in your line of sight and on target. Consciously - deliberately - move the gun randomly all over the target, being careful to keep in always within the confines of the target area. Your finger will be on the trigger; as soon as your partner gives you the command to fire ("up!") immediately - without hesitation and regardless of where your gun is within the target - stroke the trigger quickly. Recover and repeat until you've emptied the cylinder.

If you've done this correctly, all of your shots will be within the target area. (On this large target it would be unusual for them to not be within the target area.) The shots will probably be scattered within the target area; if they're in a group in the center, either you got really lucky or you weren't actually firing immediately on command. If that's the case, redo the drill.

Now repeat the drill, this time using the next smaller target. Let the gun move all it wants as long as it stays within the target area. The only difference is that now it will be moving a lot less. If you normally need to use your sights on this small target at whatever distance you're standing, use them.

Again, shoot immediately on command. If you have any shots outside of the target, which is likely to be the case, it's probably going to be due to one of the following: first, your trigger control might not be perfect and is steering the gun off of the target. Second, you may not be controlling the movement of the gun (insufficient deviation control). Third, you might be anticipating the shot and 'grabbing' it when the command is given rather than simply stroking the trigger smoothly. Finally, your stance and grasp may be weak or less than solid. Consider each one of these, make any corrections you deem necessary, and shoot it again until all of your shots land inside the target.

Shooting to greater levels of precision (as dictated by the target) is simply a case of reducing the amount of movement you allow the gun to make. You can use the smallest target or increase your distance to work on this idea, but don't go crazy - your goal is to shoot at plausible levels of precision at plausible distances. This drill is intended to teach you how to shoot to the level of precision that you need for whatever the target dictates. I shoot this drill at least once every practice session.

Volume Of Fire drill

A bad habit, particularly among competitive shooters, is always shooting double taps. (I know there is constant debate on the difference between a double tap, a controlled pair, and a hammer; I use the term double tap to denote any two shots fired in extremely rapid succession.) If you're practicing that method now, it's important that you understand why it's a bad idea - and how to break the habit.

First, as we covered previously you don't know how many rounds it's going to take to subdue your attacker. If your habit is to fire two shots then pause to fire another couple of shots, that pause is simply wasted time. It's not a lot, of course - perhaps a half second - but if you shoot a full cylinder in double taps that's a full second of time that you're not directly affecting your attacker's ability to mount a lethal threat.

Second, when I watch videos of actual attacks where many rounds are fired I don't see "bang-bang, bang-bang, bang-bang"; what I see is "bangbangbang-bangbangbang." The brain seems to know that pauses between shots serve no useful purpose and the result is typically a fast string of fire.

I've been criticized for saying this, but I think it's important to understand: the double tap is an admission to yourself that you can't control your gun in such a realistic string of fire. If you don't believe me, do this: go to the range and shoot your best double tap (fastest split time between shots). Now shoot at that same rate, but fire the whole cylinder to the same level of precision that you shot the double tap. There are very few who can do that, and I'm willing to be that you're not one of them (don't worry - I'm not, either!).

The double tap is a popular shooting cadence because it's how most of the shooting games are won: the fastest two shots that land in a target area. It's relatively easy to control the gun for two shots but it's a lot harder to do it for a string of fire, the kind that you'll probably be shooting when your life is on the line.

If you're likely to need to fire more than two shots to disable your attacker, but you can't put your third (or fourth or fifth) shot into the same target area as you did the first two, you'll need to slow down or you're going to miss. The former is unnecessary, and the latter is unacceptable.

The Volume Of Fire drill uses the large, high-center-chest area. Start at extension, with your finger on the trigger. Make sure you're in that natural, neutral stance and that you have the proper forward body weight posture; check your grasp and ensure that it's solid. On the command to fire, shoot the entire cylinder at one consistent cadence that you know will result in 100% hit accountability. Don't speed up, slow down, or put pauses between your shots;

the entire string of fire should sound like a metronome: bang-bang-bang-bang-bang-bang.

If you had a consistent cadence and all of your shots landed inside of the target area, repeat the drill but speed up a bit - say, 10% or so. If you still have 100% accuracy, speed up another 10% - keep doing this until you have a miss. The last cadence at which you had perfect accuracy is your balance of speed and precision for that target at that distance at that point in time. You should now have the confidence to always shoot at that rate when under similar conditions.

If you had some misses, correct any stance/posture/grasp/trigger control issues as we discussed above, then try again. If you still have missed shots, you now know that you can't control your gun at that cadence; slow down slightly until you have all your shots in the target.

I find that it's useful to shoot this drill at several plausible distances so that you get a very good feel for your balance of speed and precision at various ranges. It's also very important to shoot this with every revolver (or any other gun) that you expect to use for self defense, because you'll find that your cadence is different with different guns. That would be a useful thing to know before you really need to shoot!

My practice sessions usually start and often end with this drill.

PRACTICE WITH INTEGRITY

You will get out of your practice sessions only what you put into them. If you go to the range and shoot in one of the target-shooting stances or always use your sights because you can, you won't get good results for defensive shooting purposes.

I'll admit that it's hard to always shoot from a natural, intuitive position (lowered center of gravity, forward weight bias). I've found it tempting to stand up straighter and use one of the relaxed competition shooting methods, but I also realize that's not how I'm likely to respond to the sudden ambush-like attack. I force myself to do it not because it's how I shoot my best, but because it's how I'm likely to shoot when I really need to.

Shooting in a way that's consistent with your body's natural reactions is tiring. It's better to practice less but in an intuitive way than it is to shoot more but with relaxed standards. If fifty rounds are all you can shoot before fatigue sets in, then limit your sessions to that number of rounds.

Over time you'll develop the stamina to extend the length of your practice, but don't succumb to peer pressure from the folks who brag about shooting hundreds of rounds each time they go to the range. In my never-to-be-humble opinion, it's better to practice properly but less than to practice poorly but more. Stay true to your goals, to yourself, and to the context in which you expect to need your revolver.

"I LIKE TO SHOOT COMPETITION, TOO - HOW SHOULD I PRACTICE?"

As I alluded to earlier, there was a time when I shot a lot of matches - IDPA, Steel Challenge, and Bianchi Cup-type competitions. I enjoyed immensely, particularly the Steel Challenge type matches - there's something terribly addictive about that 'CLANG'!

Despite my love of competition, I gave it up largely because of my recognition that there is a difference between defensive shooting and competition shooting. That's not to say that they can't co-exist, but you will need to come to grips with the fact that those differences will affect your practice.

What is the proper balance in training and practice between them? Go back and re-read the drill about cognitive decision making. The reason we do that drill is to get ourselves to think about something other than the drawing and shooting. Our goal is to develop the recognition/recall patterns thoroughly enough that once the decision to shoot has been made, there is no need to think about the mechanics. We want the execution of our intuitive skills to be automated, and practice routines like that drill help us do that.

You'll know that the proper balance between competitive and defensive practice has been reached when you have to think about how to shoot competitively, but you don't have to think about how to shoot defensively.

What do I mean by that? When you're standing in the shooting box at a match, waiting for the buzzer to go off, if you have to consciously think about using something other than a natural, instinctive crouch; if you have to think about using your sights; if you have to think about doing your reloads the fastest way, not the most error-resistant way; if you have to think about shooting only double-taps instead of realistic strings of fire and so on, you have the proper bias toward defensive shooting.

An improper balance between those worlds occurs when you have to do the opposite: you have to think about using intuitive skills when practicing your defensive shooting. If you find yourself in defensive shooting practice having to remember to use a natural, neutral stance; if you have to think about doing your reloads efficiently, out of your line of sight so that you can focus on the threat; if you have to think about not choreographing your strings of fire - among the many other things we've covered - then you have an improper balance, one that's biased toward competition.

Does this mean your competition shooting will probably suffer? In most cases, it probably does. This brings us back to that integrity discussion: are you more interested in being an efficient defensive shooter, or a faster competitive shooter? Your answer will guide your decisions, but don't fool yourself: they are two different contexts and are quite difficult to reconcile to high standards in both.

Understand the decisions you make, why you're making them, and have the courage to stand by them.

Appendix A
RESPECTFUL IRREVERENCE

Rob Pincus wrote this piece some years ago, and it was in fact responsible for our first meeting. I read it online where it's been widely quoted, and was impressed enough to contact him and thank him for writing it.

The shooting world is full of hero worship. I have no issue with holding someone in great esteem, but if we're not careful to separate the man from his material we risk stifling our evolution. This essay is about maintaining the correct balance between admiration and deification, and I thank Rob for allowing me to reprint it here.

RESPECTFUL IRREVERENCE
by Rob Pincus

When any person, idea, technique, school, piece of gear, team or tactic is put on a pedestal, we risk stopping progress.

We should all be trying to constantly improve our own ability to achieve our goals as efficiently as possible. In the defensive/tactical world, that means becoming more dangerous to our enemies and better prepared to deal with violent conflicts. If, at any point, we decide that someone or something is beyond being questioned we will limit our ability to improve.

History is full of revered truths and experts that turned out to be wrong. Acknowledging this simple fact should remind us that today's experts and truths may be just as vulnerable to improvement.

Being open to questioning those who would be experts does not mean disrespecting them. In fact, if we look hard enough, we will probably find that our heroes themselves challenged a previously held belief or expert in order to develop their own conclusions and truths. This process is necessary for progress. I don't think anyone in the training industry has less than outstanding intentions. As instructors, however, we are all limited by the exposure we have to ideas and our ability to process them. We are limited by the type of students we have worked with, the facilities at which we've taught and the systems in which we operate.

It has been said that a 3rd year college physics major today knows more about the relationship between matter and energy than Albert Einstein did when he wrote the Theory of Relativity which describes it. In a perfect world, the students will always eventually outshine the instructors. I know that I have learned a lot from students and their feedback. Student questions have forced me to examine my own teachings more closely and sometimes change them for the better. Occasionally, feedback from students (including those who watch instructional DVDs or read articles like this one) can turn an idea on its ear and initiate a whole new approach to a problem or explanation for a solution.

I have spent a lot time over the last few years doing instructor development for civilian, military and law enforcement personnel. I want to take this opportunity to share with the readers of this blog some of the important tenets that I pass on during those courses that I think benefit us as students as well in our approach to training.

Success breeds complacency

We learn from mistakes and improve through failure. Success breeds only complacency and pride. While we love to celebrate our victories, we need to spend much more time analyzing our losses in order to find areas to improve. Training that revolves around ego building and developing a positive mental attitude tends to become a choreographed series of feel-good-drills and simplistic scenarios.

The fact that some technique has been used successfully does not mean that it is unquestionable. History is full of examples of "best ways" that were bested through innovation, experimentation and critical thinking.

Avoid absolutes

Never say never. Skepticism is an important trait in anyone seeking to improve on an existing system. Without a fair dose of skepticism, one is likely to jump on the first bandwagon that passes by. Once on-board, a failure to think critically can lead to figuratively being taken for a ride. One of the first indications of a need for questions is an absolute. If someone says "Always" or "Never," it is your responsibility to find the exception. By identifying the exception, you will improve the system and be able to better prepare. If the exception doesn't exist… look again, or be open to accepting it (and adjusting appropriately) if someone else finds it.

Ask (and answer) the "Why?" questions

"Just another tool for your toolbox" is potentially the single most damaging phrase in the training industry. Instructors owe their students more of an explanation for investing time & effort (let alone money) in a technique, tactic or principle than to just offer that it is something that might work for them.

Most instructors use this phrase not our of ignorance, they use it to avoid confrontations with Type A students who might want to argue based on previous training, they use it out of their own complacency because it has never been questioned or they might use it because they truly believe that the tactic is simply just another tool. I think the student deserves a detailed explanation as to why the instructor is teaching any given skill or concept. Intellectual Comfort with an idea is vital to efficient learning.

If the answer to the "Why?" question is "…because that's how [we/the team/some other team/this school/etc] does it!" I really suggest a long & hard deep breath, followed by extreme skepticism throughout the rest of the course. Dogma has no place in this arena. My staff instructors operate under threat of termination if they ever use this type of answer with a student.

An instructor should always teach what they truly believe to be the best option for any given situation and be ready, willing and able to explain why.

Context dictates Curriculum

Students should be taught things that will work in the context that they are likely to need them. Spouting content blindly without regard for the realities of the student is simply lecturing, not teaching. Picture the guy who stands in front of a power-point and reads it to the class. Unfortunately, this type of "instructor" is far too common and sometimes offers little to the student.

Any course outline needs to be open to adjustment to accommodate the student situations, questions, equipment and abilities. I always say that I know about 95% of what I'm going to teach at the start of any given course, the last 5% comes from student interactions and it is often some very important stuff!

If you follow these four principles as often as possible, and look for instructors who do as well, you should be able to get more out of your training time and effort. Avoiding complacency and absolutes, answering the "Why?" questions and allowing context to influence curriculum whenever you can, may not be easy. It might even bruise some egos… maybe even yours. If the attitudes of those involved are properly aimed at the goal of improving without regard for personal preferences, the irreverence does not have to be disrespectful. We should all be standing on the shoulders of the giants that have come before us in the training industry, which enables us to see farther and reach higher than they did. If we instead kneel at the feet of those giants, be they people, schools or organizations, we will fail to build on what they have established and stagnate. The dictionary defines 'irreverent' as 'lacking in respect', or 'impious'. I prefer the latter definition in this case and believe that it is possible to be respectful of people while still not worshipping any one source of information.

In short, the next time you think about your preferred source of tactical wisdom or technical expertise: Honor the men, challenge the material.

Appendix B

REFERENCES

iMiller, Rory: "Meditations on Violence", ISBN 1594391181

iiMiller, Rory, "The Four Basic Truths of Violent Assault". http://www. budoseek.net/vbulletin/content.php?147-The-Four-Basic-Truths-of-Violent-Assault

iiiMaimon, G. & Assad, J.A.: Parietal Area 5 and the Initiation of Self-Timed Movements versus Simple Reactions. The Journal of Neuroscience, 26(9), 2487-2498

ivAngell, James Rowland, "Reflex Action and Instinct". http://www.brocku.ca/MeadProject/Angell/Angell_1906/Angell_1906_o.html

vGivens, Tom: "Lessons From The Street" DVD, Personal Defense Network (2012)

viFarnam, John S.: "DTI Quips" http://www.defense-training.com/quips.html

viiAyoob, Massad F.: "The Gun Digest Book of Concealed Carry", ISBN 9780896896116

viiiPappas, Stephanie and Bryner, Jeanna: "Eyewitness Testimony Can Be Tragically Mistaken", http://www.livescience.com/16194-crime-eyewitnesses-mistakes.html

ixLaw, Bridget Murray: "Seared in our memories", Monitor On Psychology (American Psychological Association), September 2011, Vol 42, No. 8. http://www.apa.org/monitor/2011/09/memories.aspx

xVideo transcript, "About the National Institute on Drug Abuse", National Institutes of Health. http://science.education.nih.gov/supplements/nih2/addiction/videos/about/transcript-about-nih.htm

xiTaflinger, Richard F.: "Taking Advantage". Washington State University, http://public.wsu.edu/~taflinge/psych1.html

xiiTaflinger

xiiiBowen, R.A.: "Hormone Chemistry, Synthesis and Elimination", Colorado State University. http://www.vivo.colostate.edu/hbooks/pathphys/endocrine/basics/chem.html

xivBlack, Harvey: "Investigators Pinpointing Fear's Activity in the Brain". The Scientist, June 22 1998. http://www.the-scientist.com/?articles.view/articleNo/18978/title/Investigators-Pinpointing-Fear-s-Activity-in-the-Brain/

xvGrossman, Dave: "The Physiology of Close Combat", http://www.killology.com/art_psych_combat.htm

xviSilverthorn, D.U.: "Human Physiology: An Integrated Approach", ISBN 0321541308.

xviiEagleman, David M.: "Human time perception and its illusions", http://www.ncbi.nlm.nih.gov/pmc/articles/PMC2866156/

xviiiHancock, P.A. and Weaver, J.L.: "On time distortions under stress". Theoretical Issues in Ergonomics Science; Vol. 6, No. 2, March–April 2005, 193–211. http://peterhancock.cos.ucf.edu/on-time-distortions-under-stress/

xixPincus, Rob: "Counter Ambush Training", ICE Publications, 2013.

xxGigerenzer, Gerd: "Gut Feelings: The Intelligence of the Unconscious" Penguin Books, ISBN 978-0143113768

xxiPaulev-Zubieta: "New Human Physiology", Ch. 6 (excerpted) http://www.zuniv.net/physiology/book/chapter6.html

xxiiFindlay, John and Walker, Robin: "Human saccadic eye movements". Scholarpedia, 7(7):5095. http://www.scholarpedia.org/article/Human_saccadic_eye_movements

xxiiiKrauzlis RJ, Lisberger SG.: "Temporal properties of visual motion signals for the initiation of smooth pursuit eye movements in monkeys." J Neurophysiol. 1994 Jul;72(1):150–62.

xxivhttp://www.armedcitizensnetwork.org/our-journal, particularly the Larry Hickey case.

xxvLott, John and Mustard, David, interview with Kris Osborne, Fox News. http://www.foxnews.com/story/0,2933,19857,00.html

Gun Digest
WE KNOW GUNS SO YOU KNOW GUNS   THE MAGAZINE

ENTER TO WIN
NEW PRIZES BEING ADDED ALL THE TIME!

HIGH CALIBER
SWEEPSTAKES
www.GunDigest.com

ENTER ONLINE TO WIN! CHECK BACK OFTEN!

NO PURCHASE NECESSARY TO ENTER OR WIN
Open only to legal residents of the United States and the District of Columbia age 18 years or older.
However, because of state regulations, this sweepstakes is not open to residents of Rhode Island.
All firearm transfers will be conducted in strict compliance with all applicable federal, state and local laws.
Limit: One online entry per person.